# Toddler Play

# Toddler Play

*Consulting Editor*
Dr. Wendy S. Masi

*Foreword by*
Dr. Anthony D. Pellegrini

**BARNES & NOBLE BOOKS**

NEW YORK

## This edition published by Barnes & Noble, Inc., by arrangement with Weldon Owen Inc.

2004 Barnes & Noble Books
Copyright © 2004 Gym-Mark, Inc., and Weldon Owen Inc.
All rights reserved. Unauthorized reproduction, in any manner, is prohibited. Originally published in hardback in 1999.

10 9 8 7 6 5 4 3 2 1

Library of Congress Cataloging-in-Publication
data is available.
ISBN 0-7607-5897-2
Printed in Singapore.

### CONSULTING EDITOR
Dr. Wendy S. Masi

### EDITORIAL ADVISERS
Dr. Anthony D. Pellegrini
Dr. Marilyn Segal

### GYMBOREE PLAY & MUSIC PROGRAMS
Chief Executive Officer: **Lisa Harper**
Vice President of Operations: **Donald Hendricks**
Product Manager: **Lisa Biasotti**
Play & Music Sr. Program Developer: **Helene Silver Freda**

### WELDON OWEN INC.
Chief Executive Officer: **John Owen**
Chief Operating Officer & President: **Terry Newell**
Vice President & Publisher: **Roger Shaw**
Vice President, International Sales: **Stuart Laurence**

Publisher: **Rebecca Poole Forée**
Series Manager: **Brynn Breuner**
Managing Editor: **Elizabeth Dougherty**
Writers: **Mona Behan, Susan Elisabeth Davis, Christine Loomis, Genevieve Morgan**
Copy Editor: **Mandy Erickson**
Proofreaders: **Desne Ahlers, Virginia McLean, Renée Myers, Katherine L. Kaiser, Karin Mullen**
Contributing Editors: **Cynthia Rubin, Lisa Zuniga**
Indexer: **Ken DellaPenta**

Creative Director: **Gaye Allen**
Photographer: **Chris Shorten**
Business Manager: **Richard Van Oosterhout**
Art Directors: **Angela Williams, Emma Forge**
Production Director: **Chris Hemesath**
Production Manager: **Lisa Cowart-Mayor**
Production Designers: **Janis Reed, Lorna Strutt, Leon Yu, Kristen Wurz**
Production Assistants: **William Erik Evans, Lisa Lee, Joan Olson**
Contributing Designers: **Mark Paulson, Elizabeth Marken Fiorentino**
Illustrator: **Matt Graif**
Photographer's Assistant: **Mona Long**

## SPECIAL NOTE ON SAFETY PRECAUTIONS

At Gymboree, we encourage parents to become active play partners with their children. As you enjoy the enriching activities described in *Toddler Play* with your child, please be sure to make safety your priority. While the risk of injury during any of these activities is low, Gymboree encourages you to take every precaution to make sure your child is as safe as possible.

To reduce the risk of injury, please follow these guidelines: Do not leave your child unattended, even for a brief moment, during any of the activities in this book; be particularly cautious when participating in the activities involving water because of the risk of drowning; ensure that your baby does not place in his or her mouth any small objects (even those depicted in the photos) as some may pose a choking hazard and could be fatal if ingested; make sure crayons, markers, and other writing materials are nontoxic and approved for use by children under three years of age.

Throughout *Toddler Play*, we have suggested guidelines to the age appropriateness of each activity, but please assess your own toddler's suitability for a particular activity beforehand, because ability, balance, and dexterity can vary considerably from child to child. While we have made every effort to ensure that the information in this book is both accurate and reliable and that the suggested activities in *Toddler Play* are safe and workable when an adult is properly supervising, we disclaim all liability for any unintended, unforeseen, or improper application of the recommendations and suggestions featured in *Toddler Play*.

## PLEASE NOTE

To avoid showing a preference for either gender, the use of the words "he" and "his" is alternated with "she" and "her" throughout this book and generally corresponds to the gender of the toddler shown in any accompanying photograph.

# CONTENTS

**12 MONTHS**

**1**

**AND UP**

# CONTENTS

30 MONTHS
2½
AND UP

# TYPES OF ACTIVITIES

# TYPES OF ACTIVITIES

# FOREWORD

DR. ANTHONY D. PELLEGRINI

**E**ver since I began teaching in the 1970s, I have been fascinated by watching toddlers play. What a force of nature they are—so full of energy, resourcefulness, and curiosity. They always approach play with a vigor that suggests it's their life's work, which indeed it is at the ripe old age of one or two: play is a way toddlers learn about the world and prime themselves for future achievements. Watching them inspired me to make it my life's work as well, and I've now spent more than twenty-five years in the field of educational psychology, researching the influence play has on the social, emotional, and cognitive development of young children.

I now know that all play isn't equal. Watching television for hours is too passive an occupation to provide the mental and physical stimulation toddlers need; engaging them in a rigidly prescribed activity that runs counter to their personalities or play styles won't do them much good either. For play to be meaningful, children need social interaction, enthusiasm, variety, and some degree of control. They also need partners who are sensitive to their cues and will provide encouragement and affection. In other words, they need you, their parents.

Just because toddlers naturally turn to their parents—and other caregivers—as play partners doesn't mean that keeping up with these intrepid explorers isn't sometimes a challenge. Just trying to think of activities that will keep them happily busy can tax the resources of the most imaginative person. That's where this book comes in. Drawing upon two decades of experience as America's foremost provider of parent-and-child play programs, Gymboree has created a valuable tool to inspire creative and productive play sessions in the home and on family trips. The variety of activities respects a child's need for many types of play, and the flexibility of the guidelines encourages parents to tailor the games and projects to suit their toddler's own inclinations and abilities. Above all, the activities conform to Gymboree's philosophy of "play with a purpose": they are designed to foster a wide spectrum of cognitive, social, and physical skills— and they just happen to be a whole lot of fun!

I'm confident that you'll find *Toddler Play* an enriching and inspirational resource, one that you'll turn to again and again.

Dr. Anthony D. Pellegrini
Professor, Educational Psychology
University of Minnesota

# PLAY WITH A PURPOSE

**W**HETHER THEIR expressions are marked by ear-to-ear grins or brow-furrowing intensity, toddlers at play are a wonder to behold. The concentration with which they examine—and whoops! occasionally disassemble—each new object, the enthusiasm they bring to each new endeavor, and the joy they radiate as they acquire each new skill show that for these young explorers, play is serious business. It's a way of learning about their world, other people, and themselves; of testing and pushing the limits of their abilities; and of conquering everything from the physics of sand castles to the basic rules of social interaction.

These early years are ripe with unparalleled opportunities for you as a parent to unlock your child's potential. A toddler's brain is a work in progress that is profoundly influenced by her environment, and what she is now exposed to—or not exposed to—will have a lifelong impact. This might be a daunting prospect except for a few comforting facts. First, children are born primed to learn. Second, parents instinctively strive to provide the stimulation children need. And, most important, since play is a vehicle of learning for children, engaging in this task should be fun for parent and child alike.

A STRING OF BUBBLES can be a magical delight—and a dazzling demonstration of cause and effect.

COORDINATION and rhythm go hand in hand once she's picked up the beat of a catchy tune.

mirror. His language skills improve as he listens to stories and strives to communicate his needs and preferences. Early play encounters with his peers, siblings, parents, and other adults teach him how to get along with others and to respect rules and boundaries. Becoming engrossed in a variety of play activities teaches your toddler how to concentrate and persevere.

Play also provides an invaluable window to your child's personality. By playing with him—or watching him play with others—you will

## THE BENEFITS OF PLAY

Because play comes so naturally to children and seems like nothing more than simple pleasure, it is easy to overlook the many far-reaching benefits that play contributes to your child's emotional, physical, and intellectual development. Through play, a toddler learns so many vital skills—how to communicate, count, and solve problems. He hones his gross motor skills by tossing balls or climbing up a slide and polishes his fine motor skills by painting with brushes or drawing with crayons. His imagination soars as he pretends to converse on a toy telephone or dons a succession of silly hats in front of a

A SIMPLE JINGLE can be a rockin' adventure when Mom's along for the ride.

19

soon learn how he reacts to obstacles, failures, and victories. You'll see his quirky sense of humor emerge and his social skills begin to develop over time. Your toddler's manner of playing can reveal his emotions, aptitudes, and preferred learning styles—whether he's responding well to verbal instructions or visual images, for example, or if he retains information best after hands-on experiences.

Play also affords a wonderful opportunity for bonding with your toddler. When she is in a quiet mood, cuddling and looking at picture books or building an elaborate block tower with her can create a feeling of peaceful togetherness. When she's feeling a bit rowdier, a game of hide-and-seek or a beanbag toss imparts the notion that parents can be fun as well as sources of care and compassion. When you help her acquire new skills and praise her efforts, you convincingly demonstrate how you are always there to lend support and spur her progress—and countless studies demonstrate that children learn best in a loving, supportive environment. In so many ways, being your child's enthusiastic play partner creates a special closeness that will resonate throughout both of your lives.

ROLLING TO THE MUSIC lets toddlers (and moms) exercise their rambunctious sides.

RUBBER BALLS can teach a toddler worlds about distance, size, and shape.

been carefully designed and selected for developmental appropriateness. Some are classics, some are Gymboree's own innovations, but all are designed to foster the type of loving, nurturing interaction that helps a toddler learn and forms a lasting bond between parent and child.

Although playing and learning are inextricably linked, the point of these activities is not to run your toddler through a rigid battery of exercises. Instead, *Toddler Play*'s emphasis is on having fun first and foremost through activities that also happen to spur age-appropriate development in your child. These activities help build a solid foundation for all future learning. In other words, they help your toddler learn *how* to learn.

## DIFFERENT WAYS TO PLAY

This book is designed to help you make the most of the wonderful toddler years by providing a wealth of simple and diverse activities to enjoy with your child. You'll find rousing fingerplays to sing along to, art projects, bath-time activities, games with blankets, boxes, and blocks, as well as many other imaginative suggestions. There are ways to introduce children to the joys of music, to encourage muscular coordination and strength, and to build budding vocabularies. The wide variety of activities touches upon every important component of a child's physical, mental, social, and emotional skills, and each has

## READY, SET, PLAY!

Far from being rigid, the instructions in this book are intended as guidelines for loosely structured play, open to modification as you respond to your own child's particular interests and inclinations. Get things going, then step back and allow your toddler the freedom to explore and experiment as he wishes. This is key to encouraging him to work things out on his own, learn to solve problems, think creatively, and achieve self-esteem and a sense of autonomy.

Setting up a well-designed, safe play environment also contributes to his growing sense of independence and provides stimulation: deck the walls in his room with shatterproof mirrors and colorful posters, and transform the ceiling into a starry sky or an undersea fantasy with glow-in-the-dark stickers. Arrange low bookcases or tables with a rotating assortment of toddler-friendly toys, books, and art supplies, providing bins for easy sorting and storage. Place a hamper, as well as a rack for hanging up clothes, within your child's reach. Most important, don't think you need to stock up on a lot of expensive and elaborate playthings; classics such as puzzles, bubbles, puppets, blocks, tops, and balls remain versatile and engaging toddler toys.

As you become familiar with *Toddler Play,* feel free to return again and again to your child's favorite activities. Children benefit greatly from repetition. It allows them to test and refine what they have learned, and it gives them a sense of accomplishment (for more on repetition, see page 68). And don't fret if your child doesn't seem to conform to the age bands listed—if your one-year-old, for instance, is having trouble handling the beach ball in Pass the Ball or, conversely, if your two-year-old quickly memorizes

BRING ON THE NONSENSE— no song is too silly as far as your giggly wiggle-worm is concerned.

every song and fingerplay in the book. Keep in mind that each child develops at her own pace and in her own style (for more information on developmental differences, see page 44). The age bands are simply broad guidelines, and there are plenty of activities in this book to suit every child's unique needs and preferences.

So go ahead, put on your play clothes, warm up those vocal cords, and prepare to enhance your toddler's world by trying the activities suggested in the following pages. They'll help you provide a richer, more stimulating environment for your child—and a treasury of happy memories for you, your child's first playmate.

FINGERPLAYS help your itsy-bitsy spider flex her verbal as well as motor skills.

**T**HIS BOOK'S ACTIVITIES are grouped chronologically in six-month age bands that match key stages in a child's development. The age bands are general guidelines only, as there is a wide range of developmental differences among children.

## 12 MONTHS AND UP

Whether they're crawling, cruising, or walking, one-year-olds enjoy a newfound mobility that accompanies their enormous curiosity about the world. Their fine motor skills have developed to the point where they can assuredly pick up small objects and stack a few blocks. They love listening to their parents' voices, such as when reading a story or singing a song. They understand many words and respond to some simple commands; most one-year-olds also begin saying a few words of their own.

## 18 MONTHS AND UP

Children this age explore, handle, taste, and shake, rattle, and roll everything in sight. Their increasingly sophisticated gross motor skills allow them to walk, run, and climb, and their fine motor skills permit them to throw a ball and eat with a spoon. They enjoy games that engage their tactile senses and can express an appreciation of music by swaying. Their vocabulary averages more than a dozen words, and they can usually form simple two- and three-word phrases.

### 24 MONTHS AND UP

Children's strength, flexibility, and balance are stronger and surer now: they can unscrew the lid of a jar and perform other tasks that showcase their developing fine motor abilities. Their enthusiasm for music continues, and they are beginning to use their imaginations. Most two-year-olds enjoy the company of peers, although rather than engaging in joint activities, they tend to play independently side by side. They might have more than two hundred words in their vocabulary by now, and they begin to speak in simple sentences.

### 30 MONTHS AND UP

Older toddlers delight in activities that refine and challenge their physical abilities, such as running, jumping, tricycle riding, and playing catch. Their attention spans increase, and they often show a passion for classifying activities and sorting games. They also continue to hone their fine motor skills, such as holding a crayon or paintbrush. Their fluency with language grows dramatically at this age, and they catch on to the notion of abstractions, making for a rich repertoire of fantasy play.

# PLAY ACTIVITIES

**THE FOLLOWING PAGES** contain more than one hundred activities, all designed to please and challenge toddlers and make the most of their favorite time of day: the time you spend playing together. You'll find suggestions for every type of meaningful play, from funny fingerplays and nature walks to art sessions and building projects, so you can choose the activities that best suit your child's mood and interests. All these loosely structured, open-ended games can be enjoyed with a minimum amount of equipment and a maximum amount of imagination. So flip through these pages, see what new adventure you and your toddler are ready for, and let the fun begin!

# A GUIDE TO ACTIVITIES

**I**F YOU'RE LIKE most parents of toddlers, you're probably long on love but short on time. Consequently, *Toddler Play* offers a number of quick-reference features so busy parents can learn about playtime activities at a glance. The features in this book are designed to ensure that each activity is easy to find, simple to understand, and quick to implement—allowing you to spend less time reading directions and more time having fun with your child.

**Song lyrics,** chants, and rhymes appear on a yellow background and frequently include suggested hand and body motions.

**Cross-references** point to related activities your toddler might also enjoy because they are similar in topic or spirit.

**Color photographs** of toddlers (often pictured with one of their parents) demonstrate each activity featured in the book.

**Each activity** includes concise, easy-to-follow instructions as well as information on how to vary activities and, where appropriate, how to adapt them to appeal to your child as she grows.

**Age labels** show the recommended optimum starting age for each activity. This book is divided into four age ranges. (For details on the developmental stages associated with each age, see the Introduction on page 24.) The labels provide a broad guide to help you find an appropriate activity for your child, but most activities can be adapted successfully for any toddler between one and three years of age.

## PLAY WITH CLAY
### MAKING SHAPES AND SCULPTURES

**SKILL**SPOTLIGHT

**Playing with modeling clay** allows your child to experience shapes and textures in three dimensions. And manipulating the clay builds fine motor skills and strengthens the senses. Help expand your child's vocabulary by teaching her words for colors, shapes, and textures.

**MAKING YOUR OWN**

Mix 1 cup flour, 1 cup salt, 1 tablespoon cream of tartar, 1 cup water, and 1 tablespoon vegetable oil. Simmer in a pot until clay begins to pull away from the pot's sides. When cool, add 5 drops of food coloring, and knead until smooth.

**Cause and Effect** ✓
**Creative Expression** ✓
**Fine Motor Skills** ✓
**Language Development** ✓
**Sensory Exploration** ✓

Y OU MAY HAVE FOND MEMORIES of molding clay into silly shapes, and now your two-year-old is ready to dive into the colorful stuff. Purchase nontoxic modeling clay at any toy store or make a few colorful batches yourself (see the recipe for clay at left). Provide ample working space and a few safe tools, such as a rolling pin, a potato masher, and cookie cutters.
• Most young children prefer to experiment with mashing the clay into abstract shapes. Guide her in manipulating the clay by rolling it into a ball and letting her smash it. Or make a long roll that she can tear into pieces and press back together.
• Show your child how simple shapes such as circles, squares, and triangles fit together to make recognizable objects such as faces, hats, or trees.
• To store the clay, gather several airtight containers and mark each lid with the same color as the clay it contains. When she's done playing with the clay, ask her to put it away in an appropriate container.

Turn her loose with some tools and colorful clay, and watch her creativity take shape.

**RESEARCH**REPORT

**Squishing and shaping** modeling clay does more than encourage the budding artist in your child. By allowing her to handle these and other tactile delights, you're helping her develop "knowledge of how the world works and proficiency of using different materials," states Esther Thelen, a psychologist at Indiana University in Bloomington. Educational psychologist Jane Healy is another believer in the benefits of clay, sand, finger paint, and mud, which she says help refine a child's tactile ability. Healy also offers this advice to fastidious parents: "If you tend to be fanatic about cleanliness, close your eyes and imagine little [neural] dendrites branching inside that muddy hand."

190          191

**Skill Spotlights** explain the developmental focus of each activity and also contain a quick-reference checklist of its benefits.

**Making Your Own** provides suggestions on how to fashion makeshift toys and props from inexpensive, everyday materials.

**Research Reports** highlight recent scientific findings that reveal how young children develop and learn.

12 MONTHS AND UP

# PASS THE BALL

## SKILL SPOTLIGHT

**Learning to roll** or even stop a ball helps toddlers refine their gross motor skills and develop eye-hand (or eye-foot, as the case may be) coordination. Playing with balls also helps them develop a sense of timing as they attempt to figure out how long it will take before the ball reaches them.

 **EW TODDLERS** can actually catch a ball— that takes a good bit of coordination—but most love to push, kick, and grab this engaging toy. To start your toddler out on ball play, choose a flat, grassy spot outside or a cleared space inside, and sit just a couple of feet away from her. Gently roll the ball to your child and encourage her to roll it back in your direction. As she gets better at it, sit farther and farther away. Try softly bouncing the ball between the two of you, as well.

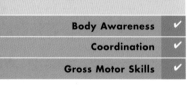

| Body Awareness | ✔ |
| Coordination | ✔ |
| Gross Motor Skills | ✔ |

If your child enjoys this activity, also try **Baby Basketball,** page 126. ▶

A BALL THAT'S ABOUT THE SIZE of your child's head is just right; it's not so big that it will overwhelm her and not so small that she'll have trouble handling it.

# THE FINGER BAND

**The Finger Band**

*to the tune of* **"The Mulberry Bush"**

**The finger band has come
to town, come to town,
come to town,
the finger band has come to
town, so early in the morning.**
*hold up and wiggle your fingers*

**The finger band can play
the drums, play the drums,
play the drums,
the finger band can play the
drums, so early in the morning.**
*pantomime playing a drum*

**The finger band can play
the flute, play the flute,
play the flute,
the finger band can play the
flute, so early in the morning.**
*pantomime playing a flute and
continue with other instruments*

**I**T'S NEVER TOO EARLY to give your toddler music lessons, especially when the instruments are make-believe. As you sing "The Finger Band" (lyrics at left), pretend to play different instruments such as drums, a flute, cymbals, and a piano. Don't worry if your child has never heard a clarinet, much less seen a trombone—she will enjoy watching and imitating your hand movements, whatever they are. Make your gestures distinct and energetic. If at first she can't copy you, move her hands and fingers for her. As she gets more coordinated and is able to imitate you, march your legs up and down as you sing and play. Try alternating between singing softly and loudly, explaining the difference as you do so.

**Eye-Hand Coordination** ✔

**Listening Skills** ✔

If your child enjoys this activity, also try **Itsy-Bitsy Spider,** page 46. ▶

PROP YOUR LITTLE MAJORETTE on your lap and introduce her to your finger band before launching into this musical parade.

# PARACHUTE PLAY

## **SKILL**SPOTLIGHT

**Parachute play** enhances your toddler's ability to balance—a skill that translates to freedom and independence, because it's a precursor to walking, running, and more complex physical actions such as skipping or even doing a somersault. Parachutes are also intrinsically interesting items to use because of their slick feel and bold colors; reinforce your child's color-recognition skills by naming the colors as you play.

| | |
|---|---|
| **Balance** | ✔ |
| **Tactile Stimulation** | ✔ |
| **Visual Discrimination** | ✔ |

**Y**OUR TODDLER WILL CHEER as you treat him to a slip-and-slide parachute ride, and you'll safely challenge his ability to balance while in motion. On a carpeted floor, seat or lay him on a colorful mini-parachute, blanket, or sheet, then gently and gradually pull him around, taking care to avoid any furniture and sharp corners as you explore the great indoors.

• Recruit another adult to help you hold the blanket or parachute over your child's head. If your child can stand with ease, test his balance by slowly raising and lowering the parachute while he stands underneath it and admires the colors or pattern. Do this motion carefully; even a lightweight parachute can topple an unsteady toddler.

• Walking in a circle, hold the blanket or parachute over your toddler's head singing "Ring Around the Rosy" (see Circle Songs, page 158, for the lyrics) or another appropriate song that your child likes. At the end of the song, let the parachute float down to the floor over your toddler. This is a particularly fun activity when a group of kids joins in the merriment.

WHO NEEDS A MAGIC CARPET?
Being transported by Daddy on a
colorful parachute, sheet, or blanket
is a toddler's dream come true.

# RHYME TIME

**N**URSERY RHYMES HAVE BEEN ENGAGING young children for centuries. Even when they don't make sense, there's something infectious and wonderful about the rhyming words. Rhymes also make language more interesting and memorable, and they help you talk to your toddler on a level you can both enjoy. Don't hesitate to create your own hand movements or gestures to complement some of the following favorite nursery rhymes.

## LITTLE BO-PEEP

Little Bo-Peep has lost her sheep and
doesn't know where to find them.
Leave them alone
and they'll come home,
bringing their tails behind them.

## HUMPTY DUMPTY

Humpty Dumpty sat on a wall,
Humpty Dumpty had a great fall.
All the king's horses
and all the king's men
couldn't put Humpty together again.

## JACK BE NIMBLE

Jack be nimble,
Jack be quick.
Jack jump over
the candlestick!

## JACK AND JILL

Jack and Jill went up a hill
to fetch a pail of water.
Jack fell down and broke his crown,
and Jill came tumbling after.

### ROUND AND ROUND

**Round and round the garden**
**goes the little bear.**
*set your toddler in front of you and run*
*your finger in a circle around his tummy*
**One, two, three, four,**
*gently squeeze each hand and foot,*
*one on each count*
**tickle under there!**
*tickle your toddler under the chin*

### LITTLE MISS MUFFET

**Little Miss Muffet sat on a tuffet**
*set your child on your lap*
**eating her curds and whey.**
*pretend to feed him from a bowl*
**Along came a spider**
*crawl your hand toward him like a spider*
**and sat down beside her**
*set your "spider" hand on his lap*
**and frightened Miss Muffet away!**
*holding your child, jump off your seat*

### HICKORY DICKORY DOCK

**Hickory dickory dock,**
*move your index fingers from side*
*to side, mimicking a ticking clock*
**the mouse ran up the clock.**
*run two fingers up your child's arm*
**The clock struck one,**
*hold up one finger*
**the mouse ran down.**
*run fingers down your child's arm*
**Hickory dickory dock!**
*mimic the ticking clock again*

YOUR TODDLER WILL LOVE to
imitate all your hand motions,
including raising a finger to
show a clock
striking one.

# BUBBLE BUSTERS

## A POP-THE-BUBBLE GAME OF CHASE

**Chasing, catching, and popping** bubbles contribute to sensory stimulation, eye-hand coordination, body awareness, and gross motor skills. And if your toddler tries to blow bubbles herself, she'll learn about cause and effect. Your bubble buster is also discovering that when she touches an apparently solid object, it sometimes pops—her first lesson in physics!

### MAKING YOUR OWN

For the soap solution, mix 1 cup of water, 1 tablespoon of glycerin (available in most pharmacies), and 2 tablespoons of dishwashing detergent. Fashion bubble wands from pipe cleaners, plastic bag ties, even plastic cups with the bottom cut out.

| | |
|---|---|
| **Eye-Hand Coordination** | ✔ |
| **Gross Motor Skills** | ✔ |
| **Language Development** | ✔ |
| **Tactile Stimulation** | ✔ |

**I**F THERE IS A MAGIC EQUATION for entrancing a toddler, it must be the combination of a simple soap solution and a bubble wand. Blowing, chasing, and popping bubbles is an excellent opportunity to encourage movement, stimulate eye-hand coordination, and introduce the concepts of big and small, high and low. Experiment with an assortment of bubble wands in varying sizes. Don't be surprised if your toddler enjoys this activity so much that "bubble" becomes one of her favorite words!

• Use a large wand to make big bubbles and cheer her as she chases and pops them, then repeat the activity with a smaller wand. Blow forcefully when you're creating a shower of tiny bubbles and softly when you're making a huge bubble. Blow the bubbles up high and down low, saying "high" or "low" as they float away.

• Take your child outdoors and blow bubbles. Explain that the wind that rustles the leaves and blows her hair also carries the bubbles away. Encourage your toddler to pop the bubbles with her fingers or stomp on them with her feet. Walk backward as you blow on the bubble wand so she'll chase you to catch the bubbles.

A BIG SHOWER OF BUBBLES will fascinate your little one. And when she chases and pops them, she'll be exercising her eye-hand coordination and gross motor skills.

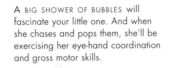

# CLAP, CLAP, CLAP

## A MOVE-YOUR-BODY SONG

**SKILL**SPOTLIGHT

**Learning the words** for body parts, and learning to control those hands, arms, and feet, is serious business for kids this age. While your toddler may already be pointing to her body parts when you name them, this song gives her a chance to practice isolating and moving her hands, feet, arms, and lips.

**I**F YOU'RE FAMILIAR with the ever-popular song "The Wheels on the Bus" (see page 57), you can add a twist to the tune with new lyrics (right). "Clap, Clap, Clap" coaxes your little one to coordinate body movements with words. Associating words and actions with a melody and a beat will help her understanding of rhythm, because she'll be able to feel it and mimic it with her body.

• Young toddlers are eager to learn the words for body parts, so be sure to emphasize those words in the song— "hands," "arms," "mouth"—by enunciating them or singing them more loudly. Make big motions at first to underscore the meaning of the words.

• Try variations: ask your child to nod her head or tap her knee, for example.

• After she's learned the song, make a few "mistakes"—clap your hands when you're supposed to be tapping your foot, for instance. Her laughter shows that she already has a sense of humor.

| Body Awareness | ✔ |
| Gross Motor Skills | ✔ |
| Listening Skills | ✔ |
| Social Skills | ✔ |

YOUR TODDLER WILL ENJOY imitating you as you clap your hands and tap your foot in this simple music game.

42

### Clap, Clap, Clap

to the *tune* of **"The Wheels on the Bus"**

You take your little hands
and go clap, clap, clap,
*clap your hands*
clap, clap, clap,
clap, clap, clap.
You take your little hands
and go clap, clap, clap,
clap your little hands.

You take your little foot
and go tap, tap, tap,
*tap your child's foot for her*
tap, tap, tap,
tap, tap, tap.
You take your little foot
and go tap, tap, tap,
tap your little foot.

You take your little arms
and go hug, hug, hug,
*hug each other*
hug, hug, hug,
hug, hug, hug.
You take your little arms
and go hug, hug, hug,
hug your mom and dad.

You take your little mouth
and go kiss, kiss, kiss,
*pucker your lips*
kiss, kiss, kiss,
kiss, kiss, kiss.
You take your little mouth
and go kiss, kiss, kiss,
kiss your mom and dad.

You take your little hand
and wave bye, bye, bye,
*wave good-bye*
bye, bye, bye,
bye, bye, bye.
You take your little hand
and wave bye, bye, bye,
wave your little hand.

# AT THEIR OWN PACE

**BABIES SIT UP** at six months. They utter their first "dada" at nine. They crawl at seven months and walk at age one. When parents are confronted by the firm developmental timetables sometimes espoused in popular child-care books, they often are pleased if their children achieve a milestone a few weeks or months ahead of schedule—and panicked if their offspring are late. But while pediatricians used to treat these timetables as if they were carved in granite, most practitioners today agree that there is a much wider developmental range in perfectly healthy children.

A child may first roll over, for example, at any time from two to six months of age. Children can vary the age at which they start talking by a year or more, and future soccer stars may take their first steps as early as eight months and as late as eighteen. Although most children follow the prescribed developmental sequence, some will skip a milestone completely—they might never learn to crawl, for example. Instead, when their muscle tone and coordination skills are ready, they simply get up and start walking.

Developmental milestones are a matter of complex neural and muscular maturation, which is affected by inherited and environmental factors—a child may walk late in life, for example, if the family has a history of late walkers. Often a child lags in one area while accelerating in another. In rare instances, a delayed milestone can signal significant problems, but in the vast majority of cases, it's just a matter of a child developing at her own rate. As educational psychologist Jane Healy says in her book *Your Child's Growing Mind*: "A child who is lagging slightly in development is on the same track as the others. His train simply goes at a slower pace, although it stands every chance of reaching the same destination." ◼

# ITSY-BITSY SPIDER

**I**N THIS POPULAR SONG, you can portray the trials of the hapless itsy-bitsy spider with fun-to-mimic hand motions. By repeating the song and the gestures you are not only entertaining your toddler but also stimulating her listening and language skills. Add tactile stimulation by crawling the spider up her tummy, "pouring" the rain down over her shoulders, and crossing her arms above her head to make the sun. When she seems proficient, try singing the song and cuing her to perform the finger movements—eventually she may surprise you with a solo.

**Itsy-Bitsy Spider**

**The itsy-bitsy spider went up the water spout,**
*walk your fingers up in the air*

**down came the rain and washed the spider out.**
*wiggle your fingers downward to make rain*

**Out came the sun and dried up all the rain,**
*form a circle with your fingers above your head*

**and the itsy-bitsy spider went up the spout again.**
*walk your fingers up again*

MIMING THE TRAVAILS of the itsy-bitsy spider not only promotes your toddler's listening and language abilities but also helps her develop fine motor skills.

✓ **Fine Motor Skills**

✓ **Listening Skills**

✓ **Tactile Stimulation**

# THE PILLOW COURSE

## SKILL SPOTLIGHT

**Movement and exploration** are near and dear to a toddler's heart, so an opportunity to move around in an interesting environment is bound to be met with joy. This activity is also an excellent way for your toddler to build his motor skills by challenging large muscle groups and to increase both his balance and coordination as he faces physical obstacles.

| Balance | ✔ |
| --- | --- |
| Body Awareness | ✔ |
| Eye-Foot Coordination | ✔ |
| Gross Motor Skills | ✔ |

 REATE A SAFE OBSTACLE COURSE in your living room or family room with a simple zigzagging path of pillows and cushions.

• Encourage your child to complete the course by crawling or walking along the path. It will be a bumpy, lumpy route, so even if he's already walking be sure to hold on to his hand as he begins the journey. Once he becomes more sure-footed, let him take some steps on the pillows by himself, but stay nearby just in case he starts to topple. Remove your toddler's shoes and socks to help him keep his balance.

• Vary the height of the path by stacking a couple of pillows. To make the course more challenging, run it under a table so he has to crawl underneath, or position pillows around the room so he must maneuver around soft furniture such as couches (avoid furniture with sharp edges).

• Use cushions and pillows of varying sizes, colors, and textures. Don't be surprised if your young athlete stops occasionally to feel the obstacles with his hands or feet. Allow him to explore, then gently encourage him to keep going.

## RESEARCH REPORT

**The wide range in age** at which children begin walking—any time from seven to eighteen months—reflects the complexity of this deceptively simple act. The mind as well as the body are involved in venturing those first steps, and it takes time for nerve cells to operate smoothly, allowing deliberate and controlled movement. A child also must build up sufficient muscle tone in his legs and hone his sense of balance and coordination, skills toddlers acquire at different rates.

HE'S ON THE WAY to walking when he follows a trail of pillows and cushions around the house— with Daddy's help, of course.

# HATS ON!

## SKILLSPOTLIGHT

**Talking to your toddler** about the hats the two of you are wearing helps expose him to new words that will someday become a part of his vocabulary. And seeing you in different hats teaches him that you're still Mommy even if you look a little different. When your child is a bit older, he'll start to enjoy role-playing with the hats, a game that will stretch his capacity for imaginative play.

| | |
|---|---|
| **Concept Development** | ✔ |
| **Language Development** | ✔ |
| **Social Skills** | ✔ |

**YOUR YOUNG ONE GRINS** when you put your baseball cap on backward. Now watch his face light up as you put a parade of special hats on his head, too. Pick up fun gear at thrift stores and perhaps in Grandma's attic. Then try it on and giggle together in front of a mirror. This is a good opportunity to help expand your child's vocabulary by using adjectives to describe the hats ("This big hat is red" or "The feathers are so soft").

• As your toddler gets closer to age two, he'll be able to revel in role-playing as he tries on different hats. Mimic special sound effects, such as an engine siren, to go with each hat.

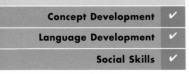

YOUR TODDLER WILL MARVEL at your elaborate headdress and smile when you make him a fire chief.

# FREEZE DANCE

## SKILL SPOTLIGHT

**By taking a ride** in your arms as you dance the night away, your toddler experiences the rhythm of music, a crucial first step in developing both language and music skills. And when you freeze in mid-action, she learns to balance herself in your arms. Suddenly turning the music on and off gives your toddler something she dearly loves—a surprise—and cultivates listening skills as well.

| | |
|---|---|
| **Balance** | ✔ |
| **Listening Skills** | ✔ |
| **Social Skills** | ✔ |

**P**LAY AN AUDIOTAPE OR CD and put a friend in charge of the volume control while you take your young dancer for a twirl—or record your own tape with sudden silences. Hold your toddler in your arms; when the music starts, exaggerate your dance moves by swaying from side to side and "dipping" her on occasion. When the music stops, hold your stance; begin dancing when the music starts again, then "freeze" each time it halts. Older toddlers may be able to dance—and stop—on their own, but most are just as happy to "freeze" in your embrace.

SWINGING TO THE BEAT of the music is a surefire way to thrill your toddler—especially when you surprise her with sudden pauses in your boogie.

# TWINKLE, TWINKLE

**S**OME SONGS ENDURE generation after generation, so parents and grandparents can share their old favorites with young children. But old favorites can be changed in new and surprising ways: as you sing these variations of "Twinkle, Twinkle Little Star," try to come up with some simple—or silly—improvisations of your own.

## TWINKLE, TWINKLE LITTLE STAR

**Twinkle, twinkle little star,**
*hold hands up, opening and closing fists*
**how I wonder what you are!**

**Up above the world so high,**
*point upward*
**like a diamond in the sky.**
*create a diamond with thumbs
and forefingers*

**Twinkle, twinkle little star,**
*open and close fists*
**how I wonder what you are!**

SHE'LL BE ENCHANTED when you sing and mime the old standby "Twinkle, Twinkle Little Star"—but there are countless variations if you want to try new lyrics.

## THE APPLE TREE

 to the *tune* of "Twinkle, Twinkle Little Star"

**Way up high in the apple tree**
*stretch arms up high*
**two little apples**
**looking down at me.**
*make circles around eyes with thumbs
and forefingers*

**I shook that tree**
**just as hard as I could,**
*shake an imaginary tree with
both hands*
**down came the apples**
*float fingers down*
**and "mmm" they were good!**
*rub tummy and smile*

**I shook that tree**
**just as hard as I could,**
*shake an imaginary tree with
both hands*
**down came the apples**
*float fingers down*
**and "mmm" they were good!**
*rub tummy and smile*

## THE SKY SO BLUE

to the *tune* of "Twinkle, Twinkle Little Star"

**Way up in the sky so blue**
*reach up to the sky with both hands*
**two little clouds said "peekaboo."**
*play peekaboo with hands*

**The wind blew the clouds**
**just as hard as it could,**
*rub hands together and shiver*
**down came the raindrops**
*flutter fingers down*
**and "oooh" . . . they felt good!**

**The wind blew the clouds**
**just as hard as it could,**
*rub hands together
and shiver*
**down came the
raindrops**
*flutter fingers down*
**and "oooh" . . .**
**they felt good!**

# THE WHEELS ON THE BUS

## SKILL SPOTLIGHT

**The catchy tune** and easy-to-follow gestures make this sing-along a skill-building activity for all toddlers. Repeating the song stimulates your toddler's auditory development, while the hand movements help him conceptualize what the words mean. As his motor skills and memory improve, he will readily imitate most of the hand gestures and even begin to anticipate many of them.

| | |
|---|---|
| **Body Awareness** | ✔ |
| **Concept Development** | ✔ |
| **Coordination** | ✔ |
| **Language Development** | ✔ |
| **Listening Skills** | ✔ |

**T**HIS SONG is an all-time toddler classic. You can perform it in many ways, but it's easiest with your child seated facing you or on your lap facing away from you. If he's propped up on your lap, gently guide his hands through the movements.

• Begin by showing him the different motions as you sing, then encourage him to join in.

• Don't hesitate to improvise your own verses and corresponding hand movements if the spirit moves you—your toddler will love it!

TAKE A FAVORITE PASSENGER for a ride on the bus, showing him how the wheels go round and round and the wipers go swish, swish, swish.

### The Wheels on the Bus

**The wheels on the bus go round and round,**
*roll forearms forward in a circular motion*

**round and round,**
*continue to roll arms*

**round and round.**
*roll arms*

**The wheels on the bus go round and round,**
*roll arms*

**all through the town.**
*draw a circle in the air*

**The horn on the bus goes beep, beep, beep,**
*press imaginary horn with hand*

**beep, beep, beep,**
*press horn with hand*

**beep, beep, beep.**
*press horn with hand*

**The horn on the bus goes beep, beep, beep,**
*press horn with hand*

**all through the town.**
*draw a circle in the air and continue with:*

**The wipers on the bus go swish, swish, swish . . .**
*sway forearms back and forth*

**The driver on the bus says "Move on back" . . .**
*point over your shoulder with your thumb*

**The lights on the bus go blink, blink, blink . . .**
*open and close fists*

**The baby on the bus goes waah, waah, waah . . .**
*make cradling motion with your arms*

**The parents on the bus say I love you . . .**
*hug your child*

# BAND ON THE RUN

## MUSIC FROM THE KITCHEN CABINET

**SKILL**SPOTLIGHT

**One way toddlers learn** cause and effect is by making sounds with a variety of objects. As a child bangs on a bowl, he learns that he is capable of creating sounds by himself. As he practices, he improves his coordination and his understanding of rhythm. As he experiments with the various "instruments" in his cabinet, he learns that he can create a myriad of interesting (and loud!) sounds.

| Cause and Effect | ✔ |
| Coordination | ✔ |
| Listening Skills | ✔ |
| Rhythm Exploration | ✔ |

 LEAR OUT A KITCHEN CUPBOARD (near the floor) and fill it with wooden and metal bowls, wooden spoons, lightweight pans (like cake pans and frying pans), metal lids of various sizes, and plastic measuring cups. The greater the variety of "instruments," the greater the variety of sounds you and your toddler will be able to make, so be creative as you stock the cupboard. If you have toy instruments on hand, add them to the mix.

• With older toddlers, create a stop-and-go band. Have your child bang on the "instruments" while listening to you—the bandleader—give directions to stop the music and start it again.

• As your young musician plays, encourage him to experiment with sound by banging in different ways: gently, slowly, fast. Be sure to demonstrate to show him the difference.

• Play one of his favorite music tapes or CDs with a strong beat and encourage him to add his own percussion sounds.

EVERYTHING BUT THE KITCHEN SINK—and that would probably work as well—is a potential instrument for a budding musician.

## RESEARCH REPORT

**The raucous noise** that results from your toddler's kitchen concert is actually good "brain food," says educational psychologist Jane Healy. "Toys with sound or visual input improve cognitive skills, but it is important that [your child] be able to interact with them. Banging two pans together is far better . . . than pushing buttons to create noises produced by hidden electronic parts. The child should be able to link cause and effect— and see the parts of the toy at work."

59

# PEEKABOO BOXES

## SKILL SPOTLIGHT

**This activity refines** your child's visual memory and fine motor skills. Most significantly, matching a word with its visual representation helps build language skills he'll need later, when he begins to read and write. As your child's vocabulary expands, surprise him now and then by pasting new pictures inside the boxes.

**C**OLLECT AN ASSORTMENT of cigar boxes, shoe boxes, or gift boxes. Cut out pictures of family members or easily recognizable objects (such as household items, animals, or toys) and paste one inside the lid of each box. Open the boxes and discuss the images inside. As your child's confidence grows, ask him to open the boxes and name the pictures. Once he masters this (around two years of age), test his memory: ask him which box contains the picture of Daddy, a horse, or a ball.

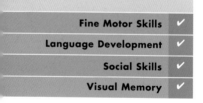

| Fine Motor Skills | ✔ |
| Language Development | ✔ |
| Social Skills | ✔ |
| Visual Memory | ✔ |

If your child enjoys this activity, also try **Picture This,** page 66.

FINDING A PHOTO of Mommy, Daddy, or the family dog under the lid of a box is a great way to boost your little one's sense of discovery while enhancing his visual memory.

# FUNNY FEET

## **SKILL**SPOTLIGHT

**Walking barefoot** is easier for your young toddler than walking with shoes because she can use her tiny toes to help with balance. And while the sensations of walking or running on unusual surfaces may make her giggle, she'll start to grasp the properties associated with different materials, as well as a few words to describe them.

| | |
|---|---|
| **Body Awareness** | ✔ |
| **Language Development** | ✔ |
| **Sensory Exploration** | ✔ |
| **Tactile Discrimination** | ✔ |

**E**VEN A CHILD who has been toddling for several months is still getting used to the sensations involved in walking. Take advantage of her curiosity by removing her shoes and leading her outside across a variety of textures, such as warm sand, smooth pebbles, cool concrete, wet grass, and gooey mud. As she gets older, ask her what she feels as she's walking. If she doesn't know the words yet, suggest some: "warm," "prickly," or "soft," for example. If you're worried about dirty feet, stomping in a basin of warm, soapy water at home will continue the game.

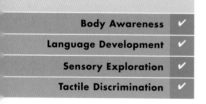

If your child enjoys this activity, also try **Bubble Busters,** page 40.

YOUR TODDLER WILL DELIGHT in the feel of different textures, such as soft grass, on her sensitive soles. Take off your shoes and join in the fun!

# CARDBOARD COTTAGES

CREATING A PINT-SIZE PLAY WORLD

## **SKILL**SPOTLIGHT

**Creeping through tunnels** fosters motor coordination and spatial awareness, while playing house and peekaboo with Mommy or Daddy encourages social skills. Choosing decorations helps older toddlers learn to discuss likes and dislikes and to express their artistic talents.

### MAKING YOUR OWN

Rectangular boxes make good tunnels; square boxes make nice cottages. Decorate the cottages with construction paper and pens to make them more homey. Just be sure to keep the "floor" of the box on the bottom so it won't collapse.

**Y** OUR TODDLER'S GREATEST JOY is trying to be independent; her greatest frustration is not being big enough, strong enough, or "allowed enough" to be all she would like to be. A town made of cardboard boxes makes a toddler the master of her own universe, and it's easy enough for you to build. Place boxes end to end to create tunnels for crawling and hiding, and use appliance or large packing boxes to make perfect playhouses.

• Cut door and window flaps in the sides of boxes so your toddler can open and shut them. Play "bye-bye" and peekaboo games as she looks out so she can practice being independent while you're still close by.

• Turn boxes into sensory centers: lay differently textured carpet scraps inside, leave musical toys in corners, and provide baskets of colorful objects to empty and refill.

| Gross Motor Skills | ✔ |
| Sensory Exploration | ✔ |
| Social Skills | ✔ |
| Tactile Stimulation | ✔ |

If your child enjoys this activity, also try **Hide-and-Seek,** page 106.

A CARDBOARD PLAYHOUSE gives
your child an independent world;
knowing Mommy is nearby lets
her explore it with confidence.

65

# PICTURE THIS

## SKILL SPOTLIGHT

**Reading is an important tool** for learning language. Toddlers learn most of the rules of grammar simply by hearing you and others speak. And recent studies show that the size of a toddler's vocabulary depends on how much speech she hears in a meaningful context. So the more you read to your child, the easier it will be for her to develop strong language skills.

| | |
|---|---|
| **Language Development** | ✔ |
| **Listening Skills** | ✔ |
| **Visual Discrimination** | ✔ |
| **Visual Memory** | ✔ |

**HE MAY NOT BE ABLE** to talk and she may not understand all your words, but even a young toddler loves to "read books" with a parent or grandparent. The rhythm of the words engages her; the pictures teach her about her world.

• Choose books with clear pictures of familiar objects and point them out to your child as you read. It will help her learn the words for everyday things, such as "chair," "house," and "car."

• Select books made of cloth, plastic, or heavy cardboard. They can withstand toddlers' eager jaws and paws more readily than paper. And small books with padded covers are easier for little hands to handle.

• Edit out long narratives and hard words. Instead, abridge the plot and spend time talking about the illustrations or photographs. This approach will help keep her interested and help her develop observational skills.

• Emphasize the rhymes and funny words that engage her.

• Tailor your reading session to her attention span. Let her wander off to play when she wants to. Ending the session while it's still fun will ensure that you're building a positive association with reading that will last a lifetime.

EVEN A CHILD who is too young to understand the plot will delight in the colorful pictures, the simple rhymes, and the cadence of Grandma's voice.

## RESEARCH REPORT

**Although teachers** often exhort parents to read to their school-age children, a report by the Carnegie Corporation found that only half of all American babies and toddlers receive this attention. Yet early exposure to these important tools of learning and pleasure, as Penelope Leach writes in *Your Baby and Child,* helps children "to make friends with [books] and learn to value them." She recommends that parents introduce their toddler to a variety of both picture and story books, and suggests they spend a lot of time talking about the illustrations. "'Reading' pictures," Leach explains, "is a necessary start toward reading text."

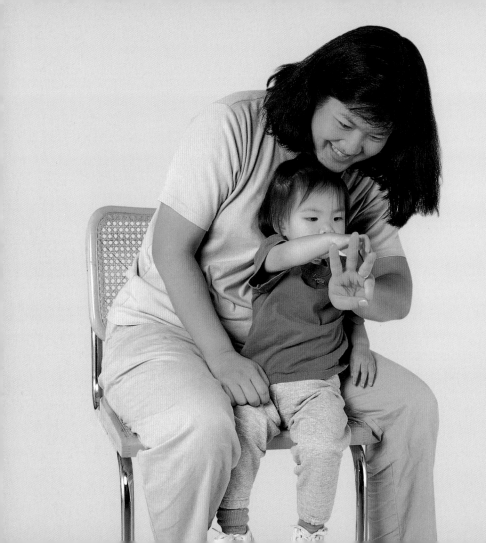

# REPETITION IN PLAY

**THINK YOU'LL GO NUTS** if you have to spend another minute rolling a ball back and forth with your toddler? Bored with reading his favorite book over and over again? Or maybe you're just worried that your child needs more variety in his play and you feel you should try to keep him from returning again and again to a few preferred activities.

Although it may try your patience, never underestimate the value of repetition when it comes to a child's development. As educational psychologist Jane Healy says in her book *Your Child's Growing Mind*, "An activity must be repeated many times to firm up neural networks for proficiency." In other words, by repeating the same story to your child every evening you are helping to stimulate the brain cells that allow your child to make the association between words and the objects they represent. And when it comes to rolling that ball, you'll soon see how your toddler's eye-hand coordination improves. A simple activity such this helps prime him for more complex tasks in coming years, whether it's understanding the nuances in James Joyce's *Ulysses* or perhaps playing a game of major-league baseball.

Besides, kids don't get bored as easily as adults do. As neurologist Ann Barnet notes in *The Youngest Minds*, "Nursery rhymes and simple games enthrall small children precisely because they become familiar." Mastering a new skill gives them a lot of confidence and even whets their appetites for future challenges.

This isn't to say that parents can't overdo it by spending too much time interacting on one activity with their child—even young minds and bodies can get overtaxed. So take your cues from your child: watch for signs of frustration or restlessness, but if he's enjoying an activity, let him do it . . . over and over and over again. ∎

A TOY INSIDE a jar provides plenty of incentive to lift off the lid.

# FUN-FILLED JARS

**C**OLLECT A FEW large, clear plastic jars with easy-to-remove lids. Place a favorite toy or colorful scarf inside each jar and close the lid. Ask your child to take off the lid and pull out the toy or scarf. (You might need to start this activity with loose lids so her not-so-nimble fingers can remove the toys more easily.) Your toddler will be eager to remove the toys over and over again. When you're filling the jars, be sure to select toys that are more than 1¾ inches (4.5 cm) in diameter (so there won't be a choking hazard).

## SKILL SPOTLIGHT

**Learning to remove a lid,** even if it's already unscrewed, helps your toddler develop coordination and fine motor skills. In addition, just attempting to unscrew a lid enhances these skills as well. In this activity, success is immediately rewarded, ensuring that your toddler will want to try removing the lids again and again.

✔ **Fine Motor Skills**

✔ **Language Development**

✔ **Social Skills**

If your child enjoys this activity, also try **Cereal Challenge,** page 108.

# SILLY LAP SONGS

**S**ITTING ON A PARENT'S LAP is not a passive activity for a busy toddler. Although your lap is a safe haven for your child—a place to relax and cuddle between activities—it's also associated with such pleasures as reading, bouncing, and singing the following songs and pretending to be an airplane, a pony, or even a frog.

MAKE YOUR TODDLER feel secure as he soars like an airplane by looking at him, smiling, and having as much fun as he is.

## THE AIRPLANE SONG

to the *tune* of "Row, Row, Row Your Boat"

**Fly, fly, fly your plane,
fly your plane up high.
Merrily, merrily, merrily, merrily,
high up in the sky!**

*hold your child firmly with both hands
and slowly raise him overhead as if he
were a flying airplane*

## DOWN BY THE BANKS

**Down by the banks of the hanky panky, where the bullfrogs jump from bank to banky.**
**They went oops, opps, belly flops.**
**One missed the lily pad and went . . . kerplop!**

*bounce your child on your lap as you teach her this chant; holding her securely, let her "slip" partway between your legs when you say the word "kerplop"*

## TROT LITTLE PONY

 *to the tune of* **"Hush Little Baby"**

**Trot little pony, trot to town,**
**trot little pony, don't slow down.**
**Don't spill the buttermilk,**
**don't spill the eggs,**
**trot little pony, trot to town.**

*holding your toddler securely on your lap, gently bounce her up and down as if she were riding a pony*

## WHEN WE ALL ROLL OVER

*to the tune of* **"Have You Ever Seen a Lassie"**

**When we all roll over,**
**roll over, roll over,**
**when we all roll over,**
**how happy we'll be!**

**Roll this way, and that way,**
**and this way, and that way,**
**When we all roll over,**
**how happy we'll be!**

*bounce your toddler on your lap as you sing, or, lying on your back, place him facedown on your stomach and rock him gently from side to side*

# I HAVE A LITTLE DUCK

MAKING WAVES WITH A SONG

**I Have a Little Duck**

*to the tune of* **"The Wheels on the Bus"**

I have a little duck that says
quack, quack, quack,
quack, quack, quack,
quack, quack, quack.
I have a little duck that says
quack, quack, quack,
all day long.
*"quack" your hands to the beat*

I have a little duck that goes
splash, splash, splash . . .
*splash the water gently*

I have a little duck that goes
swim, swim, swim . . .
*skim your hands on the surface*

| | |
|---|---|
| **Cause and Effect** | ✓ |
| **Language Development** | ✓ |
| **Listening Skills** | ✓ |
| **Rhythm Exploration** | ✓ |
| **Sensory Exploration** | ✓ |

 **HARE THIS FAMILIAR TUNE** with your child as you play in a baby pool or bathtub—and use a family of rubber ducks as colorful props. Your toddler won't need much encouragement to splash, so be sure you are both ready to get wet. In the first verse, "quack" your hands (place your palms together as if you're miming a duck bill) in the water. Little will your toddler know that in the midst of all the hilarity, you are stimulating her auditory memory and enhancing her sense of rhythm.

If your child enjoys this activity, also try **Clap, Clap, Clap,** page 42.

YOUR DARLING DUCKLING will have fun playing in the water while watching you quack and splash to the beat of this cheery song.

# JUST LIKE ME

**Just Like Me**

to the *tune* of **"London Bridge Is Falling Down"**

**Make your arms go up
and down, up and down,
up and down,
make your arms go up
and down, just like me.**
*move arms and continue with:*

**Move your hands up
and down . . .
Move your shoulders up
and down . . .
Flap your elbows up
and down . . .
Make your legs go up
and down . . .**

| | |
|---|---|
| **Body Awareness** | ✓ |
| **Concept Development** | ✓ |
| **Coordination** | ✓ |
| **Creative Movement** | ✓ |
| **Listening Skills** | ✓ |

**M**AKE THE MOST of your toddler's natural instinct to mimic with this lively activity. Give yourself plenty of room and either sit with your child on your lap or kneel facing him. Emphasize the name of each body part as you sing and point it out on your toddler's body as you make the movements. If your child is hesitant, gently help him raise and lower his arms, shoulders, and legs. Between repetitions of the song, ask him to point to his own arms or legs. Once he's following you like a pro, try adding some movements of your own invention.

If your child enjoys this activity, also try **The Wheels on the Bus,** page 56.

SHOWING YOUR TODDLER how to
make his arms go up while singing
this song is a fun way to introduce
him to the names of his body parts.

# A STAR IS BORN

**As you may have noticed,** your toddler is quite focused on herself at this stage—and with all things belonging to her. Just as a mirror intrigues her because she can see herself, a tape recording lets her revel in the sound of her voice. This helps her develop her listening skills, which are crucial to language development.

| Language Development | ✔ |
| Listening Skills | ✔ |
| Social Skills | ✔ |

**Y**OU'VE SEEN HOW your little one perks up at the sound of other children's voices. And you've noticed how she responds to seeing her face in the mirror. Now imagine her delight upon hearing a "reflection" of her own voice! Recording your child's voice gives her a whole new sense of herself and gives your entire family an audio "baby journal" to cherish for years to come.

• Record your toddler's sounds—laughing at Daddy's funny faces, babbling to herself as she plays, talking on her toy phone (see Ring-A-Ling, page 164), or shrieking with glee in the tub.

• Try recording a session the next time you read a book to your toddler so when she's older she can listen to your story-time voice and her own commentary.

• You can use a cassette recorder with a built-in microphone, but a separate microphone that can be plugged into the recorder will provide a sharper sound.

• When your young crooner is older, around age two or three, encourage her to sing several songs on tape—alone or with you or her friends if she's shy.

## RESEARCHREPORT

**Recent studies show** that the size of a toddler's vocabulary depends largely on how much her caregivers talk to her. University of Chicago researcher Janellen Huttenlocher found that 20-month-olds whose mothers had the gift of gab were shown to have about 130 more words in their vocabulary than same-age children with less talkative moms. By age two, the gap had doubled. But planting a child in front of a television won't do: the interaction between child and speaker, as well as a connection to real-life events, is necessary for all of those precious words to soak in.

ONCE YOUR STARLET understands the purpose of the microphone, she'll reach for it and talk into it enthusiastically, which allows her to experience herself in a whole different way.

# MIRROR, MIRROR

**Y**OUR CHILD has no doubt been fascinated with her own image since she was a wee baby. But mirror fun really begins in toddlerhood, because now she understands that the image is of herself—and understanding herself and all her body parts are her primary interests.

• Sit or stand with your toddler in front of a mirror and make faces—sad, happy, and goofy, for example. With an older child, encourage her to follow suit.

• Then point out her arms, legs, eyes, nose, mouth, and other body parts. Point out your own, as well.

• Ask her who's the baby and who's the mommy—pretty soon she'll surprise you by pointing to the right image.

## SKILLSPOTLIGHT

**A sense of herself as a person** (hence her intrigue with the notions of I and mine versus you and yours) is key to your toddler's development. Playing with mirrors helps her develop this concept of self as separate from others. Toddlers are also intrigued with their bodies; labeling the parts of her body in front of the mirror helps her understand the names of those parts and encourages her to further explore her own identity.

| ✔ | **Body Awareness** |
| ✔ | **Language Development** |
| ✔ | **Self-Concept** |
| ✔ | **Social Skills** |
| ✔ | **Visual Discrimination** |

WATCHING HER REFLECTION in a large mirror supports your toddler's growing awareness that she is indeed a real person, with arms, eyes, and a happy face.

81

# HEY MR. KNICKERBOCKER

**Hey Mr. Knickerbocker**

**Hey Mr. Knickerbocker, boppity, bop!**
*pat your hands flat on the floor once, clap, then repeat*

**I like the way you boppity, bop!**
*continue alternately patting and clapping to establish a beat*

**Listen to the sound we make with our hands.**
*rub palms to make a chafing sound*

**Listen to the sound we make with our feet.**
*stomp feet loudly on floor to the beat*

**Listen to the sound we make with our knees.**
*tap fingers softly on knees to the beat*

**Listen to the sound we make with our teeth.**
*click teeth together and continue with other body parts*

**S**EAT YOUR TODDLER on your lap or on the floor in front of you for this favorite chant with silly sound effects. Create a slow beat by alternately slapping your hands on the floor and then clapping them together. Encourage your child to clap with you once you begin the chant. Repeat the chant's first two lines before you make a new motion and sound. When your toddler attempts to control his body to make a specific type of sound—such as stomping his feet, clapping his hands, or clicking his teeth—he improves both his language and motor skills.

| Fine Motor Skills | ✓ |
| Gross Motor Skills | ✓ |
| Listening Skills | ✓ |

If your child enjoys this activity, also try **The Finger Band**, page 34.

ENTERTAIN EACH OTHER
with all the funny sounds
you make while reciting
this favorite chant.

83

18 MONTHS AND UP

$1\frac{1}{2}$

# PAPER-BAG BLOCKS

## SKILLSPOTLIGHT

**Children enhance** their fine motor skills and their ability to discriminate among shapes and sizes when they explore and play with blocks. Most kids also love to practice stacking the blocks—then knocking them down, of course. That provides a good lesson in balance, as well as in cause and effect. And if your budding architect builds a little fort or cave, having a private space that's just his size can bolster his emerging sense of identity.

| Cause and Effect | ✔ |
| Fine Motor Skills | ✔ |
| Problem Solving | ✔ |
| Size and Shape Discrimination | ✔ |
| Spatial Awareness | ✔ |

**A**T THIS AGE, his hands may be too small to skillfully maneuver heavy wooden blocks. But you can make large, lightweight blocks from paper bags and milk cartons that are both easy to handle and soft on impact.

• To make large blocks, fill a paper grocery bag to the brim with crumpled newspaper. Fold and tape the sides of the open end as if you were wrapping a present. Help your child decorate the oversize blocks using non-permanent markers, crayons, wrapping paper, or stickers.

• For smaller blocks, thoroughly rinse and dry empty milk cartons. Open the tops and vertically cut through the corner creases to create flaps. Tape the flaps shut and cover the cartons with colored construction paper or even contact paper with a brick motif (to create a "brick" house).

• Now let your kinder-contractor begin to build. Encourage him to stack the blocks as high as he can or to use them to create little forts. Furniture such as a couch or a table and sheets can provide additional walls and a roof.

• Also show him how to stack the small blocks on top of the big blocks to build a toddler-size tower. When it's time to disassemble the stack, take turns removing one block at a time, and count the blocks out loud as you remove them. Then create new structures with your little builder.

PLAYING WITH PAPER BLOCKS helps
your young architect learn how
to stack objects and increases
his understanding of size,
shape, and balance.

# SIZE WISE

**SKILL**SPOTLIGHT

**A nesting game** keeps toddler minds and hands busy as they learn to recognize differences in size. It also helps children learn to solve problems ("How do I get these to all fit together?") and enhances eye-hand coordination and fine motor skills. The give-and-take between parent and child is important, too: your toddler is learning to listen and let you show her how to do things.

**Y**OUNG TODDLERS frequently derive endless pleasure from taking objects out of a container and then trying to put them back again. Increase the complexity and fun of this type of activity by introducing your child to nesting objects, which require her to fit things together in a particular order.

• You can buy nesting containers at toy stores. You can also use measuring spoons, mixing bowls, or cardboard boxes of different sizes for the same effect.

• Some toddlers do not yet have the manual dexterity to get the objects to nest or to pull them apart again. Start out slowly by introducing your child to this activity with only two or three nesting cups that vary dramatically in size. Demonstrate how the items fit within each other. You may need to show her several times, but eventually she'll be able to help you; then she'll figure out how to nest the objects on her own.

• Gradually add to the number of nesting objects once she has mastered fitting the first few cups or bowls together.

| Eye-Hand Coordination | ✔ |
| Fine Motor Skills | ✔ |
| Problem Solving | ✔ |
| Size and Shape Discrimination | ✔ |

NESTING BOWLS TOGETHER teaches your toddler some important lessons about size differences while satisfying her curiosity about your shiny kitchenware.

## RESEARCHREPORT

**A toddler's ability** to sift through a jumble of cups and bowls and sort them into piles by shape or size demonstrates the dawning of logical reasoning. As exciting as it is to see a child master the simple but important concepts of same and different, it's obviously still a long journey to the type of sophisticated thinking associated with higher forms of logic. Jonas Langer, a psychologist at the University of California at Berkeley, notes that a child's logical powers make a big jump in complexity between the ages of four and eight, but she isn't able to truly comprehend notions of abstract symbolism until she reaches age eleven or so.

# HIDE YOUR EYES

**Hide Your Eyes**

 to the *tune* of **"The Farmer in the Dell"**

**Can you hide your eyes,
can you hide your eyes?
Yes you can, you surely can,
you can hide your eyes.**
*cover your eyes with your hands*

**Can you hide your nose,
can you hide your nose?
Yes you can, you surely can,
you can hide your nose.**
*cover your nose with your hands*

**Can you hide your feet,
can you hide your feet?
Yes you can, you surely can,
you can hide your feet.**
*cover your feet with your hands*

*Continue with chin, knees, toes,
elbows, ears, and so on.*

| Body Awareness | ✔ |
| Creative Movement | ✔ |
| Language Development | ✔ |

**T**HIS SING-ALONG takes a toddler favorite—the peekaboo game—and applies it to several parts of your child's body. In turn, this activity helps your toddler learn the words for many of her body parts as well as how to sing along with others.

• Kick off the "Can You Hide Your Eyes?" song with the names of some easy body parts, such as eyes, nose, feet, and toes. Then graduate to less familiar words, like elbows, knees, chin, and neck.

• Make a few "mistakes" once in a while to see if she catches them—cover your knees when you say "toes," for instance, or cover her knees instead of yours. She'll be amused by these silly contradictions.

90

YOUR CHILD GETS TO PLAY peekaboo while singing when you add these new lyrics to an old, familiar tune.

91

# SHAKE IT UP, BABY!

## SKILLSPOTLIGHT

**Playing with musicmakers** stimulates auditory reflexes and nurtures a child's innate sense of rhythm, both of which are fundamental to language development. Identifying various kinds of sounds helps train the ear to recognize pitch and volume, while dancing and shaking or playing the instruments will encourage creative expression. If you make your own maracas, provide your child with additional tactile stimulation by allowing her to feel the rice, beans, and pennies before you put them in the bottles (but make sure she doesn't try to eat them).

INTRODUCE YOUR CURIOUS CHILD to new sounds and rhythms by supplying her with child-size maracas or other percussion instruments (available in most toy stores). Or create your own little musicmakers by filling a few small plastic bottles with rice, dried beans, or pennies. Close the lids tightly and seal them with packaging tape to prevent any spillage (items under 1¾ inches, or 4.5 cm, in diameter are choking hazards). Begin by shaking each instrument or bottle, then pass it to your toddler, commenting on the unique sound it makes. Play a selection of familiar songs with different tempos and encourage her to make music and move her body to the beat.

| Creative Movement | ✔ |
| Listening Skills | ✔ |
| Rhythm Exploration | ✔ |
| Sensory Exploration | ✔ |

If your child enjoys this activity, also try **Rhythm Time,** page 120.

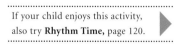

A FEW HANDMADE INSTRUMENTS
and a good song are all your toddler
needs to let the rhythm move her.

MOST TODDLERS ARE THRILLED to play in a pile of sand; add to their fun by showing them how to make designs with sand toys and kitchen utensils.

# SAND SKILLS

**Z**EN MASTERS DO IT. Bulldozers do it. And toddlers can do it, too. Whether you're at the beach, on a playground, or in a backyard sandbox, making designs in the sand is absorbing, creative, and entertaining. It also provides a great way to combine artistic endeavors with healthy outdoor play.

• Gather a variety of tot-size tools, including sand toys (plastic buckets, shovels, and molds), kitchen utensils (spatulas, wooden spoons, and plastic containers), and garden tools (watering cans and miniature rakes).

• Pour water over the sand to make a more pliable palette.

• Show your child how to use the tools to make designs. He can draw a rake through the sand, for instance, to create straight or wavy rows of lines. Or he can press a pie pan into the sand to make a big circle. Use empty yogurt containers and wet sand to add towers and turrets.

• Show your toddler how he can erase his creations by dumping water on top of them or by simply running his hands over the sand. Then encourage him to build again.

**SKILL**SPOTLIGHT

**Sand is wonderful** for artistic explorations because it allows a toddler to safely wallow in the medium from head to toe. Grasping and releasing the sand and using a variety of tools to manipulate it also exercise his fine motor skills and stimulate his sense of touch.

| ✔ | **Creative Expression** |
| ✔ | **Fine Motor Skills** |
| ✔ | **Tactile Stimulation** |

# PHOTO FUN

## PUTTING NAMES TO FACES

**Your toddler picks up** the rules of grammar by hearing your speech patterns. But she can't learn who Cousin Emily is or what an ostrich looks like just by listening. She needs a picture to put a face to a name. This flash-card activity helps expand her vocabulary, which in turn helps her organize and share her memories.

### MAKING YOUR OWN

Tape or glue photos to playing cards or index cards. For extra protection from enthusiastic little hands, laminate the cards or have a copy or framing shop do it for you. To hang, use tape or large magnets; avoid thumbtacks and small magnets.

I T MAY SEEM LIKE your toddler has nothing but a Be Here Now (or Give It to Me Now) perspective on life. But she's been able to store and retrieve memories since she was about six months old. Now she's driven to remember and practice saying the names of people and objects around her. Flash cards add fun to memorizing.

• Tape or glue photos of family members and friends to index cards (this will enable your child to pick them up more easily). Point to someone in a picture and say the person's name. Pretty soon she'll be calling out their names even before you do.

• Glue photos to a piece of construction paper and laminate it for a "personalized" place mat.

• Using photos cut out of magazines, make cards depicting appealing things that aren't already in her daily life, such as an anteater, giraffe, or helicopter. Hang the cards at eye level (on the refrigerator, for example) and point them out to her often.

• Attach stories to the images so your toddler will have an easier time remembering them. You can say, "We made cookies with Grandma, didn't we?" This helps her learn how to tell stories, and it shows her that people are interested in them. It also helps her mentally process familiar events.

| Language Development | ✓ |
| Visual Discrimination | ✓ |
| Visual Memory | ✓ |

HELP YOUR CHILD sharpen her memory skills by filling her world with images of familiar faces and asking questions such as "Where's your Uncle Virgil?"

97

# THE MAGIC OF MUSIC

**THE HUMAN PASSION** for music is a universal trait, a gift parents from every culture naturally bestow on their children. We coo lullabies as babies drift off to sleep, clap as toddlers make their first wobbly forays onto the living-room dance floor, and play endless games of patty-cake with our youngsters. Which is a good thing: recent studies, such as the one outlining the much-publicized Mozart effect detailed on page 157, suggest that exposure to music has far-reaching intellectual benefits that go way beyond just imparting a sense of melody and rhythm.

Mark Tramo, a neuroscientist at Harvard Medical School, explains that the same mental pathways used to process music also seem to serve as conduits for language, math, and abstract reasoning. "This means that exercising the brain through music strengthens other cognitive skills," Dr. Tramo concludes. The governor of Georgia, among many others, found this evidence so compelling that he decided to send every baby born in Georgia home from the hospital with a recording of classical music.

This book includes simple and enjoyable suggestions for filling your child's world with the sound of music, from the tape-recorded parent-and-child duets on page 78 to the percussion games on page 120. Many of the activities link movement with music, which helps your toddler assimilate language and rhythm, develop coordination, and heighten body awareness. Complement these exercises by listening to a variety of music—while driving, eating, or doing chores or art projects, for example—and you'll further enhance her auditory senses and broaden her musical horizons. Don't feel you have to play classical music if that's not your favorite: introduce your child to the tunes you enjoy, and your pleasure can make her only more receptive to the value and power of all music. ■

# TAMBOURINE TIME

## MAKING MERRY MUSIC

**Simple musical instruments** offer toddlers a rich variety of activities that both stimulate and fine-tune auditory and tactile senses. As children play and listen, they begin to discriminate among different rhythms and types of sounds. And a tambourine, which can be either tapped or shaken, reinforces what toddlers are already discovering: that the world is full of unique and varied sounds—sounds they not only can recognize but also can produce all by themselves.

| | |
|---|---|
| **Eye-Hand Coordination** | ✔ |
| **Listening Skills** | ✔ |
| **Rhythm Exploration** | ✔ |
| **Social Skills** | ✔ |

**T**HE TAMBOURINE IS MUSIC to your toddler's ears, arms, fingers, toes, and just about any other body part. Give him a tambourine and encourage him to shake it and tap it to the beat of his favorite songs—or to accompany you if you play an instrument. Move around as you play. Experiment with some tambourines of different sizes: how do the sounds of large and small ones compare? How does the sound change when you shake the tambourine hard, then shake it gently? The two of you can delight in each other's musical discoveries.

If your child enjoys this activity, also try **Shake It Up, Baby!**, page 92.

THE JINGLE AND THE JANGLE
of a toy tambourine can teach
a toddler a lot about sounds.

# CRAYON CREATIONS

## SKILL SPOTLIGHT

**Grasping and using a crayon** builds fine motor skills and eye-hand coordination. It also can help a child learn to identify colors. More important, letting him express himself by choosing his colors and scribbling in whatever way he pleases allows him to give color and shape to his budding sense of identity. Discussing what the two of you are doing as you draw helps cement concepts in his memory and develop his communication skills.

| Concept Development | ✔ |
| Fine Motor Skills | ✔ |
| Social Skills | ✔ |
| Visual Memory | ✔ |

 **EVEN CHILDREN** as young as eighteen months are thrilled to put crayon and pen to paper. It can be hard for them to aim, however, and difficult to understand that the crayons or markers need to stay inside the paper's edges (and not on the table or floor). Rather than fence your child in with standard letter-size paper, let him spread his artistic wings to create mural-size artwork.

• Clear a large area on the floor and tape down poster-size sheets of paper. Sit next to your toddler, hand him some non-permanent markers or crayons, and encourage him to scribble on the paper. You may have to show him how at first, but once he gets going, he won't want to stop.

• Talk about what you're doing as you draw. When he picks up a crayon, tell him what color it is. Encourage him to use different colors and praise whatever marks he makes on the paper.

• With an older child, ask him to describe what he is drawing. If he's drawing a circle or square, for example, identify the shape and explain that it's round like a ball or square like a box. Control your desire to help him make perfect shapes. His drawings may look like only a bunch of squiggly lines to you, but they're masterpieces to him.

OVERSIZE CRAYONS AND MARKERS are easily gripped in the chubby fingers of your artist-in-the-making. Watch to see if he already has a couple of favorite colors!

# COUNT WITH ME

**Y** **OUR TODDLER** is always happy to hear you sing, but songs and chants that emphasize counting add educational fun. While your child will love just to listen to you, she'll also begin to recognize numbers. Repetition reinforces the learning, so sing an encore or two.

**Five little raindrops falling
from a cloud,**
*wiggle fingers on one hand
downward*

   **the first one said,
   "My, the thunder's loud."**
   *hold up one finger; cover ears*

   **The second one said,
   "It's so cold tonight."**
   *hold up two fingers; shiver
   and hug body*

**The third one said,
"Oh, the lightning's so bright."**
*hold up three fingers; cover eyes*

**The fourth one said,
"Listen to the wind blow."**
*hold up four fingers; cup hand at ear*

**The fifth one said,
"Look, I'm turning into snow."**
*hold up five fingers; float fingers down*

**So down they tumbled through
the cold winter's night,**
*roll arms downward in front of body*
**and turned all the earth to
a frosty, snowy white.**

COUNTING RAINDROPS, caterpillars, and crayons is a fun way to introduce your child to the concept of numbers.

## THE CATERPILLAR

**One little caterpillar crawled
on my shoe.**
*wiggle finger like a worm on a shoe*

**Along came another and then
there were two.**
*show two fingers*

**Two little caterpillars crawled
on my knee.**
*wiggle two fingers on knee*

**Along came another and then
there were three.**
*show three fingers*

**Three little caterpillars crawled
on the floor.**
*walk three fingers across the floor*

**Along came another and then
there were four.**
*show four fingers*

**Four little caterpillars all crawled
away.**
*walk four fingers across the floor*

**They will all turn into butterflies
one fine day!**
*flap your arms like a butterfly*

## TEN LITTLE CRAYONS

 to the *tune* of "Ten Little Indians"

**One little, two little, three little
crayons,
four little, five little, six little
crayons,
seven little, eight little, nine little
crayons,
ten little crayons in a box.**
*hold up one finger for each crayon
as you count them*

**Take out a red one and
draw a big circle.**
*draw a circle with your finger*

**Take out a blue one and
draw a straight line.**
*draw a straight line*

**Take out a yellow one and
draw a little triangle.**
*draw a triangle*

**Then put them
back in the box!**
*pretend to replace
them in the crayon box*

# HIDE-AND-SEEK

## A FOLLOW-THE-VOICE GAME

**T**HEY START WITH PEEKABOO when they're babies; later they'll startle you by shrieking "Boo!" as you turn the corner. In between, there's this sweet game of hide-and-seek designed just for a toddler.

• When your child's attention isn't focused directly on you, find a nearby tree, chair, or wall that you can hide behind. Call out to your toddler: "I'm hiding, try to find me!" As he searches, urge him closer with your voice. Soon he'll learn to follow the sound of your voice until he finds your hand, leg, shoulder, and, finally, your beloved face. Give him a congratulatory hug and play the game again.

• Teach him to hide so you can seek him out. He'll mostly hide his head, forgetting that you can see his little legs sticking out from behind the bed or his fingers clutching the blanket. But make a big show of pretending you don't see him. Then act surprised when you happen to find him.

"WHERE'S DADDY? Oh! There he is!"
A rousing game of hide-and-seek
stimulates your toddler's curiosity
and eases his separation anxieties.

### SKILL SPOTLIGHT

**Following the direction** of a sound, such as Daddy's voice, teaches children to listen carefully. And as your child learns that the part of you that's sticking out—whether it's your shoulder or your feet—is attached to the rest of you, he'll strengthen his visual memory.

| ✔ | Concept Development |
| ✔ | Listening Skills |
| ✔ | Social Skills |
| ✔ | Visual Discrimination |
| ✔ | Visual Memory |

# CEREAL CHALLENGE

## SKILL SPOTLIGHT

**This deceptively simple activity** promotes learning problem-solving techniques and demonstrates the concepts of in and out as well as the principle of cause and effect. Once your child has mastered this challenge, raise the stakes with this visual memory game: take three plastic yogurt or margarine containers and hide cereal in one of them. Mix them up, then urge her to find the one with the cereal (also see Magic Cups, page 180).

F IND A BOTTLE that's clean, unbreakable, and small-mouthed (a plastic baby bottle or water bottle works well). Drop some of your toddler's favorite breakfast cereal into it. Show your toddler the cereal in the open bottle and ask her to get it out. Allow her to experiment, but if she becomes overly frustrated, demonstrate how to tip the bottle over. Increase the challenge by lightly screwing on the top or asking her to drop the cereal back into the bottle. To further fine-tune her motor skills, try this with a variety of containers that have different types of lids.

| | |
|---|---|
| **Cause and Effect** | ✔ |
| **Concept Development** | ✔ |
| **Fine Motor Skills** | ✔ |
| **Problem Solving** | ✔ |

If your child enjoys this activity, also try **Size Wise**, page 88.

BOTTOMS UP! There's nothing like a snack to motivate your budding genius—just watch how quickly she catches on.

18 MONTHS AND UP
$1\frac{1}{2}$

109

# SHAPE TO FIT

## SKILL SPOTLIGHT

**The ability to classify** as well as discriminate among sizes and shapes is a fundamental skill that not only helps toddlers make sense of the world but also prepares them for activities they'll encounter in play groups, camps, and preschool. Sorting, grasping, and fitting shapes promotes the development of fine motor skills and eye-hand coordination, which will in turn aid toddlers as they practice using forks and spoons, manipulating toys, and coloring.

| | |
|---|---|
| **Classifying Skills** | ✔ |
| **Eye-Hand Coordination** | ✔ |
| **Fine Motor Skills** | ✔ |
| **Size and Shape Discrimination** | ✔ |

 **HICH SHAPES GO WHERE?** Toddlers love a mystery, and this is one they can solve with some help from you. Use a shape-sorter toy or cut out three or four simple shapes on the tops and sides of some sturdy cardboard boxes. (Make sure the shapes are about the same size so the triangle won't fit into the hole for the circle, for instance.) Ask your toddler to drop the shapes into the matching holes. Demonstrate the activity to get your child started, then let your young detective work on this visual mystery at her own pace. It may take some time before your child is able to easily discriminate among shapes, but most children this age enjoy practicing.

If your child enjoys this activity, also try **Magnet Magic,** page 138.

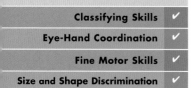

MATCHING UP SHAPES teaches more than geometry; a child also learns how to solve new challenges.

# POINT OUT THE PARTS

## SKILL SPOTLIGHT

**Identifying and repeating** the names of body parts plays a role in language development; not only is your child learning to match your real nose to the word "nose," she's also feeling what a nose is by touching it or sniffing with it. The resulting physical sensations increase her awareness of her body and her body parts.

| | |
|---|---|
| **Body Awareness** | ✔ |
| **Concept Development** | ✔ |
| **Language Development** | ✔ |
| **Listening Skills** | ✔ |

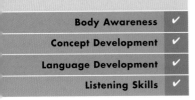

**L**ABELING BODY PARTS is an important first step in your child's sense of herself as a separate person. This simple activity aids the process of self-discovery, which begins at the end of the first year of life and blossoms in the second. Learning and saying the names of body parts also sharpens your toddler's verbal skills and memory, and increases her awareness of her body.

• To start, sit facing your child and touch her nose. Then take her finger in your hand and guide it to your nose. Say "nose" several times as you tap her finger on your nose. Then ask her to point to her own nose. Continue with other body parts, such as head, arm, leg, and foot. It may take her a while to distinguish between "Mommy's nose" and "baby's nose"— that's natural. But eventually this will become a favorite game of hers and one that gives her a sense of accomplishment.

• If she has the verbal skills to say some of the names of the body parts, ask her to repeat them as you point to them. Or initiate a movement game that shows her how to shake her head, stomp her foot, and wiggle her tiny toes.

KNOWING THE DIFFERENCE between Mommy's hair and her own mouth is a major milestone for a proud pointer. Next, talk about how her hands are small and yours are big.

# NATURE ART

## CREATING A NATURAL COLLAGE

**SKILL**SPOTLIGHT

**Letting your child choose** her own objects (a red flower versus a yellow one, for instance) and arrange them herself helps her identify and express her personal preferences. Talking to her about nature as you explore the outdoors encourages her to notice and describe the world. And the task of applying objects to paper, especially a sticky contact sheet, helps enhance her fine motor skills.

| | |
|---|---|
| **Creative Expression** | ✔ |
| **Eye-Hand Coordination** | ✔ |
| **Fine Motor Skills** | ✔ |
| **Language Development** | ✔ |

**T**ODDLERS LOVE THE OUTDOORS, love to collect things, and love to dabble in the arts—as you've no doubt noticed with your child's oatmeal finger paintings at breakfast time or perhaps her crayon murals. Nurture this trio of passions by helping your toddler create a collage of natural elements.

• Take her on a walk in your backyard, a park, or the woods and collect leaves, flowers, grass, sticks, feathers, and whatever else she finds that appeals to her (and is safe to handle.)

• Expose your child to some new words and concepts by talking about what you find ("See this feather? That's from a blue jay." "Look, the flowers are turned toward the sun.").

• Once you're home, place a piece of clear contact paper, sticky side up, on top of a cookie sheet with a rim. Tape each corner of the contact paper to the cookie sheet to keep the paper from sticking to your hands.

• Help your child arrange her treasures on the contact paper.

• Place another piece of transparent contact paper, sticky side down, over the first one to help preserve your toddler's work.

PRESSING BACKYARD TREASURES between contact paper is a creative way to cultivate a love of the Great Outdoors.

115

# WATER THE PLANTS

**Water the Plants**

*to the tune of* **"The Mulberry Bush"**

**This is the way we
water the plants,**
*put one hand on hip and bend
the other like a curved spout*
**water the plants,
water the plants.**

**This is the way we
water the plants
whenever they get dry.**

**We water the plants
so they will grow,**
*crouch down on the floor,
then slowly stand up*
**they will grow,
they will grow.**

**We water the plants
so they will grow
way up to the sky.**
*raise your hands skyward*

| Balance | ✔ |
| Coordination | ✔ |

**T**HIS GARDENING SONG will teach your toddler a fundamental lesson about nature: that plants need water to grow!

• Show your child how to tip way over as he "pours" the water from his "spout." That's good balance practice. If he likes rowdier play, pick him up and tip him over instead.

• Reinforce the gardening lesson by asking him to help you water some real plants, either inside or outside. He will enjoy both participating in your chores (see Copycat, page 250) and nurturing living things.

◀ If your child enjoys this activity, also try **Hide Your Eyes,** page 90.

TWISTING LIKE A SPOUT gives your little one a handle on what makes gardens grow.

117

# SURPRISE!

## SKILL SPOTLIGHT

**Unwrapping an object** requires solving problems and having nimble fingers. Playing with different patterns and textures stimulates a child's visual, tactile, and auditory senses, especially when the paper crinkles or pops as he handles it.

| | |
|---|---|
| **Coordination** | ✔ |
| **Problem Solving** | ✔ |
| **Sensory Exploration** | ✔ |
| **Tactile Discrimination** | ✔ |

**F**OR MOST TODDLERS, the wrapping paper on a present is at least as fun as the gift itself. They love the brightly colored paper, the noise it makes when they crinkle it, and the challenge of discovering what's inside. Your child can enjoy this activity any day of the year if you gather several of his favorite toys and books and wrap them loosely in colorful paper (no tape) while he watches.

Show him one package at a time, asking, "What's inside the paper?" Let him remove the wrapping—but lend a helping hand if he gets frustrated. Wad up the paper while commenting on the sound it makes and how it feels.

If your child enjoys this activity, also try **Peekaboo Boxes,** page 60.

THE ACT OF UNWRAPPING is fun, stimulates the senses, and helps develop coordination.

18 MONTHS 1½ AND UP

119

# RHYTHM TIME

## SKILL SPOTLIGHT

**Your child is born** with an innate sense of rhythm. But learning to pound out a beat—especially while practicing with you—lets her see how it fits into music, dance, and other rhythmic activities. Drumming also enhances her eye-hand coordination, and learning to vary the pace and volume fine-tunes her muscle control.

| Cause and Effect | ✔ |
| Creative Expression | ✔ |
| Listening Skills | ✔ |
| Rhythm Exploration | ✔ |

### MAKING YOUR OWN

Creating a drum is as simple as turning over a saucepan or wooden bowl. Try wooden, metal, and plastic spoons for varying sound effects; use different-size containers to create varying pitches (the smaller they are, the higher the pitch).

**Y**OUR CHILD ALREADY KNOWS how to make plenty of noise by banging her spoon on the table, clapping her hands, and pounding on the door she wants opened. You can direct this energy toward more musical pursuits—as well as encourage her sense of rhythm—by showing her how to bang out a beat with a drum.

• Buy a drum with a couple of mallets (or make your own). Sit with your child and show her how to hit the drum with either a mallet or her hand. Demonstrate how to hit the drum softly, then loudly. Try varying the pace of the drumming so she experiences fast beats as well as slow ones.

• Put on some lively music and demonstrate how to drum to the beat. Don't expect her to follow the music exactly—that will come when she's older. Sway back and forth, tap your foot, clap your hands, and toss your head from side to side to show her other ways of expressing rhythm. Or get your own drum and pound out a noisy duet.

SHOW YOUR LITTLE DRUMMER GIRL the different sounds she can make, then let her march to her own beat.

18 MONTHS · $1\frac{1}{2}$ · AND UP

# TODDLER PARADE

## MAKING A SPECIAL DAY WITH EVERYDAY TOYS

**SKILL**SPOTLIGHT

**This is the very beginning** of fantasy play: she's pretending to be a member of the parade and she's mentally converting her toys (and her parent) into appropriate props. Walking (or even marching) to music will help her learn rhythm. And she'll develop new levels of coordination by figuring out how to pull her little pretend-parade behind her.

 **VERYONE LOVES A PARADE**, but you don't have to wait for a holiday or struggle with crowds to let your toddler participate in one. Instead, create a pint-size parade in your own home, complete with music, celebrities (albeit fuzzy ones), and an emcee. Make your child the grand marshal of the event.

• Help her collect her wheeled toys in the "staging grounds" (for example, your living room). Tie the toys together with short lengths of string so she can pull the makeshift contraption behind her. If you have a toy wagon, prop stuffed animals inside to serve as famous folk. To get really fancy, decorate the "floats" with streamers. You could even make confetti!

• When your toddler gets a little older, play lively marching music, outfit yourself with a drum (a spoon and a pot will do) or a fake baton, and start parading around with your child in tow. She probably won't be able to march and pull her toys at the same time, so pull the floats for her while she practices stepping high and swinging her arms.

NOTHING CAN RAIN on her personal parade when she has her rolling elephant, horse, and lion marching with her.

| | |
|---|---|
| **Creative Expression** | ✔ |
| **Fine Motor Skills** | ✔ |
| **Gross Motor Skills** | ✔ |

## RESEARCH REPORT

**In studies conducted** in the United States and Britain, psychologists Anthony Pellegrini and Peter K. Smith showed that children instinctively seem to understand the importance of play and freedom of movement. When their free play was restricted for a period of time, the "deprivation led to increased levels of play when opportunities for play were resumed," the psychologists concluded. In other words, when finally let loose, the kids tried to make up for lost playtime.

123

# PLAYING WITH SIBLINGS

**PLAYING ONE-ON-ONE** with a toddler lets you easily adapt to your child's needs and desires. But when you introduce a sibling into the group, dynamics change dramatically, calling for a parent to exercise a bit more imagination and a lot more diplomacy.

Several factors can complicate the situation: toddlers aren't always keen on sharing their parents' attention, even with a beloved brother or sister. If there's more than a two-year gap in ages, just finding an activity that suits both children can be a challenge. Then there are different play styles to consider: one child may be the quiet type who prefers to play alone with blocks, while her dynamo of a sister likes nothing more than to help her build block towers— before knocking them down. No wonder a session of family fun can leave you feeling more like a referee in a particularly fierce World Wrestling Federation match than a play partner.

Still, there are many ways to ensure smoother, more enjoyable play sessions. Taking into account the children's ages and personalities, devise activities that will be fun for both and accommodate different play styles. Art projects such as drawing with sidewalk chalk or painting, for instance, can be enjoyed by toddlers and young school-age children alike. Going to a playground outfitted with a variety of equipment allows children to play together for a while, and then pursue individual interests. And don't forget to stock up on duplicate toys and supplies when possible; having two sets of watercolors and two rainbow-colored balls has saved many a parent from sibling meltdown. It's also important to dole out attention in fairly equal measures. While it's natural to pay more attention to the younger child, as she might need more help, remember to offer words of praise or encouragement to the older sibling. ■

# BABY BASKETBALL

## SKILL SPOTLIGHT

**When your child** practices aiming, he improves his eye-hand coordination and gross motor skills. If you count the balls out loud as your toddler throws them into the containers, you'll help lay the foundation for understanding numbers. Whether your child is tossing the ball into a basket or at you, actively participate by gently throwing the ball back to him and encourage him to take another (more difficult) fundamental step: learning to catch.

| | |
|---|---|
| **Eye-Hand Coordination** | ✔ |
| **Gross Motor Skills** | ✔ |
| **Social Skills** | ✔ |

 ATHER A FEW MEDIUM-SIZE BALLS and place them in a large container such as a laundry basket or a cardboard box. Show your child how to empty the balls onto the floor; then demonstrate how to drop the balls one by one into the basket. Initially, your toddler may enjoy simply putting the balls in the basket and taking them back out. When he's ready, have him stand back and try throwing the balls into the basket. Increase the challenge by placing a few containers around the room, then urge your athlete to aim toward a different one each time.

If your child enjoys this activity, also try **Tube Tricks,** page 130.

ALL YOUR YOUNG DRIBBLER NEEDS to practice his eye-hand coordination and motor skills is a ball, a "basket," and an enthusiastic coach!

# THE NOBLE DUKE OF YORK

## SKILL SPOTLIGHT

**Your toddler** is beginning to form a clearer sense of himself as an object in space. This song game—while fun to play with a parent—helps him learn the meanings of spatial words, such as up, down, and over. And while your child may not be quite old enough to tell right from left, he'll get the idea, at least, that those words refer to something other than straight ahead.

| | |
|---|---|
| **Concept Development** | ✔ |
| **Language Development** | ✔ |
| **Spatial Awareness** | ✔ |

**Y**OUR CHILD'S UNDERSTANDING of the concepts of space and movement increases slowly but surely in the toddler years. If your child loved lap songs as a baby, he'll probably get a big kick out of this more advanced version, which teaches him just some of the ways he can move about in the world.

• As with all song games, enunciate the sounds clearly and emphasize the corresponding movements to help teach your toddler the meaning of the most important words. Those emphases also create a song with more drama and vigor, which makes it more exciting for the two of you.

• As your toddler gets older, he can sing this song standing on the floor instead of sitting on your knees. Try marching during the first stanza, then stretching up and crouching down in the second stanza. With the third stanza, have him drop to the floor and lie on his back, then gently push his legs left, right, and up in the air.

If your child enjoys this activity, also try **The Choo-Choo Train,** page 132. ▶

THIS FUN TUNE—bolstered by Mommy's bouncy movements—helps your little duke learn about moving up and down.

**The Noble Duke of York**

**The noble Duke of York,
he had ten thousand men,**
*bounce child on your knees,
facing outward*
    **he marched them
    up to the top of
    the hill,**
      *march your legs
      upward with child
      still on knees*
    **and he marched
    them down again.**
      *march your legs down-
      ward with child still
      on knees*

**And when you're up,
you're up.**
*raise both legs*
**And when you're down,
you're down.**
*drop both legs*
**And when you're only
halfway up,**
*raise both legs halfway
up and pause*
**you're neither
up nor down.**
*move legs up and down quickly*

**He rolled them over left,**
*lean to the left*
**he rolled them over right,**
*lean to the right*

**he rolled them over
upside down,**
*lie backward with child lying
on top of you*
**oh, what a funny sight!**
*return to original position*

129

# TUBE TRICKS

## SKILL SPOTLIGHT

**Balls and disappearing acts,** as well as repetition, fascinate children at this age. But it's not just fun and games. Dropping balls into a tube and then catching or chasing them exercises your toddler's fine motor skills and eye-hand coordination. Fitting different-size balls into the tube helps her sort shapes in her mind. Taking turns dropping and catching the ball promotes sharing.

| | |
|---|---|
| **Cause and Effect** | ✔ |
| **Fine Motor Skills** | ✔ |
| **Size and Shape Discrimination** | ✔ |

### MAKING YOUR OWN

You can find tubes of all sizes at hardware stores, hobby stores, art galleries, photo shops, and the post office. Any soft balls that fit in the tube will work: tennis balls, racquet balls, or balls made of cloth, soft rubber, or foam.

**I**N ONE END AND OUT THE OTHER. It seems simple to us, but to a toddler it's like playing hide-and-seek with a ball, which is sure to puzzle and thrill her. Even when she's mastered the mystery ("Where did the ball go? There it is!"), she'll want to play this game again and again.

• Start with a wide plastic or cardboard tube and a supply of tennis, racquet, or other soft balls. Put the balls in one end of the tube, tilt the tube so they roll down inside it, and have her retrieve them from the other end. Repeat several times; then have her put the balls in and you catch them.

• Increase the complexity by using balls of different sizes. Which ones fit in the tube? Which ones don't? Be sure to choose balls that are at least 1¾ inches (4.5 cm) in diameter so they're not a choking hazard.

• You can turn this activity into a coordination exercise by asking her to catch a ball as it's falling out of the tube. You stand up and drop a ball through the tube. She waits at the bottom end of the tube, and as the ball pops out, she tries to grab it. The smaller the ball, the greater the challenge.

A CLEAR TUBE lets her watch the blue balls roll all the way from top to bottom; an opaque tube will add an element of surprise to the game.

18 MONTHS
1½
AND UP

# THE CHOO-CHOO TRAIN

## AN EXCURSION IN RHYME

**The Choo-Choo Train**

*Sit facing your child and hold both of her hands.*

**Here comes the
choo-choo train
coming down the track.
First it's going forward,
then it's going back.**
*pull one hand toward you while pushing the other toward your child; continue to alternate*

**Now the bell is ringing:
ding, ding, ding!**
*ring imaginary bell*

**Now the whistle blows:
whoo, whoo, whoo!**
*pull imaginary whistle cord*

**What a lot of noise it makes**
*cover both of your ears*
**everywhere it goes!**

| Language Development | ✔ |
| Rhythm Exploration | ✔ |

**T**ODDLERS DON'T NEED A MELODY to sense rhythm: they can feel "beats" with simple chants. When you add appealing rhymes, fun movements, an ever-friendly train theme, and an enthusiastic parent, you've got an activity that will keep your little one chugging merrily along. While you chant "Here comes the choo-choo train," play up the rhythm so your eager engineer can hear it and mimic it with her body. Ham up the movements, too. Emphasizing the gestures will help your child understand the meaning of the accompanying words.

If your child enjoys this activity, also try **Train Trips**, page 150.

THIS CHANTING GAME teaches your little conductor to feel a beat and understand the basics of forward and backward motion.

18 MONTHS
1½
AND UP

# TANTALIZING TEXTURES

## A BOOK OF SENSATIONS

**SKILL**SPOTLIGHT

**A texture book** lets your toddler discover a variety of different materials and helps him learn concepts such as rough, smooth, bumpy, and even squishy. The book can also give your child a chance to express his preferences: Does he like the scratchy feel of burlap? Or does he prefer the crinkliness of the foil?

| Language Development | ✔ |
| Tactile Discrimination | ✔ |
| Tactile Stimulation | ✔ |

**H**E'S ALREADY DETERMINED to get his hands on everything in (and out of) sight, including dollops of jam, dead bugs, and months-old cereal bits. Let his fingers experience the world safely by introducing him to a book filled with tactile adventures. You can buy a texture book for children or make your own.

• To create a texture book, collect a variety of materials, such as cloth, burlap, foil, wax paper, and bubble wrap. Glue a large square of each material onto cardboard or construction paper. Then tie with string or tape the sheets together.

• When you explore the book with your toddler, describe the different sensations you both are feeling.

If your child enjoys this activity, also try **Sand Skills,** page 94.

BOOK PAGES made of unusual textures, such as fine sandpaper or fake fur, let your child explore the world from the safety of your lap.

135

# TREE TALK

## SKILL SPOTLIGHT

**Learning all about trees** and the animals that live in them is an important step toward understanding nature in its many forms. Discovering an interest in—rather than a fear of—creepy-crawly creatures provides an essential building block for the development of compassion and an early appreciation of the wonder of natural science.

| Language Development | ✓ |
| Sensory Exploration | ✓ |
| Visual Discrimination | ✓ |

 **W**HETHER YOU LIVE IN A CITY, a suburb, or the country, your toddler is probably already drawn to all things treelike. You can encourage this natural affinity by spending time in leafy neighborhoods, parks, or forests and helping him discover the tremendous beauty of botanical life.

• Show him leaves, trunks, roots, and branches. Encourage him to explore the roughness of the bark, the smoothness of the leaves, and the gnarled contours of the roots. Also ask him to listen (for rustling leaves or birdcalls) and to smell (rich soil and fragrant blossoms, for instance).

• Look for creatures that inhabit the trees, including squirrels, birds, and bugs. Point out their homes, such as the bird's nest.

• Explain the importance of respecting all forms of life, even the little creeping ones. To help him with this, show him a harmless critter (a snail or pill bug, for example) up close.

• Name a few types of trees and explain how he can identify them. ("See the white bark on that one? That's a birch tree. But the tree with the green needles is a pine tree.")

GIVING YOUR TODDLER a Daddy's-eye view of a tree's tender leaves helps him learn to appreciate nature.

## RESEARCH REPORT

**If your child** seems particularly adept at telling oak leaves from maple and has no trouble telling a ring-tailed lemur from a raccoon, he might be exhibiting what renowned Harvard psychologist Howard Gardner calls "naturalist intelligence." Gardner, who had previously identified seven other kinds of intelligence (linguistic and logical-mathematical, for example), defines naturalist intelligence as the ability to recognize and classify flora and fauna. "Someone with a high degree of this intelligence," he says, "is comfortable in the world of organisms and may well possess the talent of caring for, taming, or interacting subtly with a variety of living creatures."

137

# MAGNET MAGIC

## PLAYING WITH TOYS THAT "STICK"

**MAKING YOUR OWN**

Create personalized magnets by gluing or taping photos of family members onto inexpensive, flat magnets. Or attach photos, drawings, or magazine pictures of your child's favorite animals. Photo stores carry magnetized photo frames, as well.

**M**ANY CHILDREN display their manual dexterity by pulling magnets off the refrigerator—and then crowing delightedly over their finds. You can make magnets even more fun by using them for a variety of games that engage your child's eyes and memory, as well as his curious fingers.

• Gather several colorful magnets and place them on a metal cookie sheet (note: magnets won't adhere to aluminum sheets). Use magnets with images of objects your toddler likes, such as animals, flowers, food, storybook characters, and cars. Avoid magnets that are smaller than 1¾ inches (4.5 cm) in diameter because they pose a choking hazard. And make sure the magnet has a well-defined edge so your child can pick it up easily.

• Ask your toddler to take the magnets off the sheet—then ask him to put them back on. Talk to him about the colors, sizes, and characters he sees on the magnets. Encourage him to move them around to create his own designs.

• With an older toddler, try removing a magnet from the sheet and asking him to guess which one is missing.

YOUR TODDLER is far too young to understand magnetic attraction, but learning that certain objects adhere to a cookie sheet is the very beginning of scientific discovery.

YOUR CHILD will enjoy playing the creepy-crawly tickling game with her fingers—especially when Mommy is an active participant.

# OPEN SHUT THEM!

## A TICKLING RHYME AND CHANT

**T**ODDLERS HAVE A GREAT LOVE for their own little bodies—and the names of their own little body parts. They also enjoy tickle and surprise games. This chant gives your child a chance to show off her knowledge of her body and at the same time play a creepy-crawly tickle game. Start out by demonstrating the chant's gestures on yourself and see if she can follow along. If she seems confused, do the fingerplay on her instead—until she is ready to copy your movements.

**Open Shut Them**

**Open shut them,**
*open and close fists*
**open shut them,**
**give a little clap, clap, clap!**
*clap three times*

**Open shut them,**
*open and close fists*
**open shut them,**
**put them in your lap, lap, lap!**
*pat lap three times*

**Creep them, crawl them,**
**slowly creep them,**
**right up to your chin, chin, chin!**
*walk fingers from chest to chin,*
*tickling your child along the way*

**Open wide your little mouth,**
*touch lips with a finger*
**but do not let them in!**
*quickly run fingers down to lap,*
*tickling your child along the way*

| ✓ | **Creative Expression** |
| ✓ | **Fine Motor Skills** |
| ✓ | **Language Development** |

If your child enjoys this activity, also try **Hide Your Eyes,** page 90.

24 MONTHS AND UP

# BEACH-BALL CATCH

## A TOSS-AND-CATCH BALL GAME

**SKILL**SPOTLIGHT

**Playing a game of catch** with a toddler is a fun and simple exercise in socialization that builds gross motor skills and eye-hand coordination. Successful catches demand quick reflexes and good spatial awareness, which may take a while for your toddler to achieve. By enthusiastically supporting your child in her attempts to catch, you are teaching her to appreciate being part of a game in a noncompetitive way.

**M**OST TODDLERS are able to throw a ball before they can catch one. But they love trying to wrap their little arms around airborne balls, and with a healthy dose of patience and practice, you can help your toddler learn the basics of catching. Begin by rolling a ball to her and asking her to roll it back to you (see Pass the Ball, page 32). When she's ready to try catching, use a slightly deflated beach ball (it's easier for small hands to grasp).

• Kneel or sit a couple of feet apart and ask your toddler to throw the beach ball to you. Demonstrate how to catch, then toss the ball to her and ask her to catch it. Once she accomplishes this (it will take a lot of practice), increase the distance between you, little by little.

| | |
|---|---|
| **Eye-Hand Coordination** | ✔ |
| **Gross Motor Skills** | ✔ |
| **Social Skills** | ✔ |

YOUR CHILD WILL CATCH ON more quickly if you show her how to grab the ball before you toss it her way.

# BALANCING ACT

## SKILL SPOTLIGHT

**Just like logs and low walls,** balance beams present an irresistible challenge to curious young children. As she perfects her walk along the beam, her ability to balance increases, and she develops crucial eye-foot coordination—skills that will help her as she moves from walking to running, jumping, hopping, skipping, and—who knows?—maybe even perfecting a gymnastic dismount.

**ATTEMPTING TO BALANCE** on narrow walkways is a natural and universal activity for young children, so you probably won't have to do much to encourage your child to try. You can find beams low enough to walk on safely at gyms, parks, and playgrounds.

• Demonstrate how to walk across, then hold your child's hand as she tries to walk slowly on the beam.

• If your toddler is reluctant at first, place a toy at the other end of the beam and encourage your young gymnast to hold your hand and walk across to retrieve it. Be sure she practices this balancing act above a soft or cushioned surface.

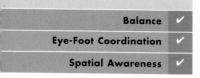

| | |
|---|---|
| **Balance** | ✔ |
| **Eye-Foot Coordination** | ✔ |
| **Spatial Awareness** | ✔ |

If your child enjoys this activity, also try **Footstep Fun**, page 174.

SHE'LL BE SURE-FOOTED in no time with her favorite coach by her side for support.

# PUPPET PLAY

## SKILLSPOTLIGHT

**By the age of two,** your child is attributing all sorts of human traits to his toys; he considers them his best friends. By making puppet toys act more like humans, you stimulate his imagination. And by telling stories and conversing with him, you accelerate his back-and-forth conversational skills.

**C**HILDREN ADORE PUPPETS because they're toys that seem to magically come to life. They'll love them even more when you put on a live, slapstick show. You can buy some fancy puppets—or just use brightly colored felt-tipped pens to draw a face on a sock or a bag. You can even tape ears or horns on your homemade puppet and glue "hair" made of yarn to its top.

• Make a stage by draping a blanket over the back of a chair or a safety gate—or position yourself behind a sofa. With one or two puppets, tell your child stories and sing songs. Try using a different voice for each puppet.

• Ask your child questions with the puppets and encourage him to converse. Question him about his favorite foods, his toys, or his mommy and daddy. And ask him to show the puppet his nose and toes—toddlers love to point these things out.

| Imagination | ✔ |
| Language Development | ✔ |
| Social Skills | ✔ |

If your child enjoys this activity, also try **Play Aquarium,** page 160.

A BIG, FAT FROG and a polka-dotted duck can share some pretty funny stories with their little human friend.

# TRAIN TRIPS

## AN IMAGINARY LOCOMOTIVE

**SKILL**SPOTLIGHT

**In this activity,** your little engineer enhances her upper body muscle coordination and learns to move with the rhythm of a chant. Puffing along as your pint-size passenger, she develops whole body coordination as well as balance—after all, it's hard to stay seated on Mommy when you're busy giggling like crazy. Role-playing also greases the gears of the imagination.

| | |
|---|---|
| **Coordination** | ✔ |
| **Gross Motor Skills** | ✔ |
| **Imagination** | ✔ |
| **Social Skills** | ✔ |

**Y**OU CAN HARNESS your child's abundant steam power by taking her on an imaginary train trip. Announce your destination ("First stop, Mommy's lap!"), pretend to pull the whistle ("Whoo whoo!"), then invite her to sit on your lap. As you chant "chug-a-chug-a-choo-choo," push her hands in a circle (like the rolling train wheels) or help her blow the whistle. Alternatively, you can both "chug" around the house ("Next stop, your bedroom!") with your child as the engine and you as the caboose.

• Pretend to navigate around curves by bending both of your bodies from side to side. Go through "tunnels" (don't forget to duck your heads!) and stop from time to time to let passengers off at the "depot."

• Sing a favorite train song or chant (see The Choo-Choo Train, page 132) while you chug around the house together.

• To help a toddler appreciate trains and enjoy this activity even more, take her to a real train station—or even the subway—and show your young conductor what it's like to ride the rails.

If your child enjoys this activity, also try **Drive the Fire Truck,** page 184.

SHE'LL EXPAND her locomotor skills and blow off a good bit of steam in this vigorous lap game.

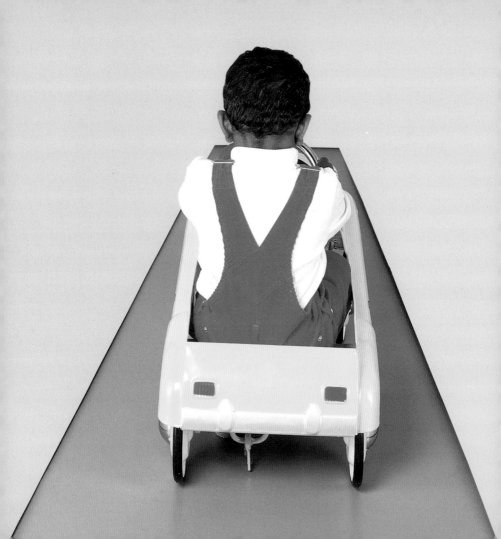

# THE "NO" STAGE

**A BIG SHOCK** for first-time parents is the transformation of their easygoing, compliant infants into mercurial toddlers whose favorite word seems to be no—"no bath," "no bananas," and "no songs," for example—even though they never seemed to mind these things before. As Dr. Benjamin Spock wrote in *Baby and Child Care*, "When you suggest something that doesn't appeal to them, they feel they must assert themselves . . . . Psychologists call it 'negativism.'" While admitting that this spell of negativism can test the resources of even the most patient parents, Spock also noted that this stage is an important signal that children are maturing into independent human beings who can think for themselves.

Being calm, cooperative, and reasonable with your toddler is one of the most effective ways to teach him to be a calm, cooperative, and reasonable person himself—but it will take time. Until he learns more self-control, you can expect temper tantrums when he doesn't get his way. It's best to ignore such behavior—if possible—to convey that he can't get what he wants in this unseemly manner. In *Raising Good Children*, developmental psychologist Thomas Lickona advises parents to keep toddlers happily busy, offer diversions when they get restless, and allow lots of free play in safe settings. He also recommends counting, such as saying, "Let's see if you can get in your chair by the time I count to ten." Another strategy is to present a child with alternatives. If he insists on wearing weather-inappropriate clothes, you could pick out two other suitable outfits and say, "Which would you like to wear today?" Such maneuvers might seem transparent to adults, but they are wonderfully effective in making a headstrong toddler feel a measure of the control and freedom he so desires. ∎

153

# PONY RIDES

## SKILLSPOTLIGHT

**Sure, a two-year-old can walk** pretty well. But that doesn't mean her balance is fully developed. As you pretend to be a pony and crawl and wiggle your way through the house, your child is learning how to find and keep her center of gravity. She's also stretching her imagination by pretending that she's riding a bucking buckaroo—or a dashing steed.

 **HE'S FASCINATED BY PICTURES** of horses, but a wee bit wary of the real thing. Give her a leg up on balance skills by playing the pony part yourself. Get down on your hands and knees and let your child "ride" on your back or shoulders. Have her hang on tight, and be ready to grab a leg if she starts sliding.

• If you want to add music, sing a song such as "Trot Little Pony" (see page 73 for the lyrics) as you crawl. To help her learn to adjust her balance, lower your upper body to the floor, raise it (not too high!), or wiggle from side to side.

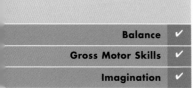

| | |
|---|---|
| **Balance** | ✔ |
| **Gross Motor Skills** | ✔ |
| **Imagination** | ✔ |

If your child enjoys this activity, also try **Footstep Fun**, page 174.

GIDDYAP DADDY! You can start your little cowgirl's riding lessons early by doing some of the legwork in your living room.

24 MONTHS AND UP

155

# HEAD TO TOES

**Head to Toes**

*Touch the body part with both hands as you sing its name.*

**Head, shoulders, knees, and toes.**

**Knees and toes!**

**Head, shoulders, knees, and toes.**

**Knees and toes!**

**Eyes and ears and mouth and nose, head, shoulders, knees, and toes.**

**Knees and toes!**

| | |
|---|---|
| **Body Awareness** | ✔ |
| **Gross Motor Skills** | ✔ |
| **Listening Skills** | ✔ |
| **Rhythm Exploration** | ✔ |
| **Visual Memory** | ✔ |

**Y**OU MAY REMEMBER THIS SONG from your own childhood, when you sang it at camp, in school, or with your friends or parents. It's also a great tune for helping toddlers learn—and remember—the names of body parts.

• Sing "Head, shoulders, knees, and toes" to your child and place both hands on your body parts as you call out the corresponding name of each part.

• Keep singing the song over and over, increasing the tempo each time. You'll probably both get mixed up and a bit breathless toward the end—but that's part of the fun!

• Is your toddler having trouble keeping up? Try touching her body as you sing; this will help her learn how the words and motions fit together.

TOE-TOUCHING TO THE MUSIC puts your toddler in tune with her body parts and the beat.

156

### RESEARCH REPORT

**Not only does music soothe** the savage beast, it seems to perk up the mind as well. Physicist Gordon Shaw and psychologist Frances Rauscher made worldwide headlines with a research study showing that college students who listened to Mozart's Sonata for Two Pianos in D Major for ten minutes before a test of their spatial-temporal reasoning ability averaged an eight- or nine-point jump in scores. This finding, along with other studies, so impressed Florida legislators that they enacted the "Beethoven's babies law," requiring state-funded day-care centers to play classical music for thirty minutes every day. While "Head to Toes" is a far cry from Mozart, Rauscher believes that any complex music (be it classical, jazz, or rock) might enhance brain development.

157

# CIRCLE SONGS

 **HESE PERENNIAL FAVORITES** are a perfect choice when your toddler has the urge to move. Best of all, there's a camaraderie that comes with circling, singing, and holding hands—whether with Mommy and Daddy or a few cherished friends.

## RING AROUND THE ROSY

**Ring around the rosy,**
*hold hands and walk in a circle*
**pocket full of posies,**
**ashes, ashes,**
**we all fall down!**
*fall to the ground*

**The cows are in the pasture,**
*remain seated in the circle*
**eating buttercups,**
*pretend to eat*
**thunder, lightning,**
*pound hands on the floor*
**we all stand up!**
*stand up quickly*

CIRCLE SONGS give your toddler a dizzying array of tunes to move to and supportive hands to hold.

## THE MULBERRY BUSH

Here we go round the mulberry bush,
*hold hands and walk in a circle*
the mulberry bush,
the mulberry bush.
Here we go round the mulberry bush,
so early in the morning.

This is the way we clap our hands,
*clap hands while standing in a circle*
clap our hands,
clap our hands.
This is the way we clap our hands,
so early in the morning.

This is the way we stamp our feet . . .
This is the way we turn around . . .
This is the way we twist and shout . . .
This is the way we reach and
stretch . . .
This is the way we run and run . . .
This is the way we sit right down . . .
This is the way we wash our face . . .

## LOOBY LOO

Here we go looby loo,
*hold hands and walk in a circle*
here we go looby light,
here we go looby loo,
all on a Saturday night.
*jump up with arms extended skyward*

## POP GOES THE WEASEL

All around the cobbler's bench,
*holding hands, run in a circle*
the monkey chased the weasel,
the monkey thought
it was all in fun,
POP goes the weasel!
*jump up, then fall to the ground*

# PLAY AQUARIUM

FUN WITH FAKE FISH

**A pretend aquarium** gives your child a chance to learn about fish and their strange habits: they swim to get around, after all, and they don't breathe air. Playing out a pretend sequence with her plastic fish gives her an opportunity to exercise her imagination. It also provides a rich environment for expanding her vocabulary to include words for colors, shapes, textures, and movements.

| | |
|---|---|
| **Creative Expression** | ✔ |
| **Imagination** | ✔ |
| **Language Development** | ✔ |
| **Sensory Exploration** | ✔ |

**M**OST ADULTS ARE CAPTIVATED by watching fish swimming in a tank. Toddlers like to watch, too, but they seem equally compelled to reach right in and grab a fistful of water, fish, or plant life. You can indulge that desire (and keep the fish safe!) by taking your child to an aquarium that offers touch pools for kids. Or you can create a customized pretend aquarium that your child can play with in her own living room.

• To make a "tank" for your toddler, place a thin layer of blue paper in the bottom of a plastic storage box or dish tub and add large shells, big plastic fish, and fake aquarium plants. Encourage your child to explore the aquatic habitat; talk about textures and colors and how fish swim, glide, and hide. Consider replacing the blue paper with bona fide water if she (and you) are ready for some wet, splashy fun. Also provide her with scoops and strainers for "cleaning" the aquarium.

• Consider setting up a real aquarium—with your child's help—if she's really interested in fish (and be sure to explain that real fish can't be held or taken out of the tank). Or take her on field trips to local pet stores to view their aquariums; she'll see various types of fish, turtles, frogs, and salamanders.

A PRETEND FISH TANK provides the perfect entrée to the wonderful wet world of a real aquarium. And this fish doesn't mind being high and dry!

161

# SCARF TRICKS

## SKILLSPOTLIGHT

**A two-year-old** is biologically driven to practice gross motor movements of all kinds, such as running, kicking, jumping, and rolling. This activity gives her a new object with which to practice throwing and catching: a silky, fluttering scarf that is as engaging to watch as it is to touch.

| | |
|---|---|
| **Eye-Foot Coordination** | ✔ |
| **Eye-Hand Coordination** | ✔ |
| **Gross Motor Skills** | ✔ |

**S**HE MAY HAVE ALMOST MASTERED catching a rolling ball, a wobbling plastic lid, or the family cat. Here's something altogether different to challenge your toddler's eye-hand coordination. Gather some brightly colored, lightweight scarves. Scrunch up a few of them simultaneously in your hand and throw them high in the air, then ask your child to try to catch them as they float and flutter toward the ground. After a few rounds, let her throw some of the scarves while you take a turn at nabbing them midair. As she gets older, encourage her to spin around or clap her hands before trying to catch the scarves.

PLUCKING A RAINBOW OF COLOR from the air is as visually stimulating as it is physically challenging.

162

"THIS IS CHRISTINA. Can you play today?" A pretend phone call with Grandpa or Auntie Elizabeth helps your budding socialite learn the give-and-take of conversation.

# RING-A-LING

**T**ODDLERS ARE DRAWN to telephones like bears are drawn to honey. But rather than shooing your two-year-old from your carefully programmed cordless telephone, give her a phone of her own. You can use a castoff from your basement, or buy a fancy toy phone (some even have push buttons that beep!). Encourage her to use it by holding the receiver to her ear and asking simple questions, such as "What are you doing today?" and "May I talk to your daddy, please?"

If your child enjoys this activity, also try **Doll Talk,** page 196.

## SKILL SPOTLIGHT

**Learning to hold a conversation,** even if it's an imaginary one, helps children exercise their emerging language and social skills. This activity is also a useful way to introduce basic phone etiquette (asking "Who's calling, please?" or replying "I'm fine, thank you," for example) before your toddler starts picking up your phone and talking to your callers.

| | |
|---|---|
| ✔ | **Creative Expression** |
| ✔ | **Language Development** |
| ✔ | **Self-Concept** |
| ✔ | **Social Skills** |

165

# BEANBAG BOWLING

**SKILL**SPOTLIGHT

**Throwing beanbag toys** or balls at targets helps toddlers develop their eye-hand coordination and adds to their understanding of cause and effect. This activity also helps your child learn to take turns, a skill he'll work on throughout his early years. Taking turns will be crucial to later social interactions, when children need to share (especially at school) to get along with others.

| | |
|---|---|
| **Balance** | ✔ |
| **Cause and Effect** | ✔ |
| **Eye-Hand Coordination** | ✔ |
| **Gross Motor Skills** | ✔ |

**W**HETHER IT'S PUSHING HIS FORK off his high-chair tray or pulling your CDs off the shelves, your toddler delights in putting objects in motion—just to see what will happen (and often to see how you'll react). This is a natural way for toddlers to learn about cause and effect. It's also a good way for children to learn about concepts like gravity and force (not that they need to learn those words—at least not yet). If you're concerned with concepts like "object fragility," however, channel your child's curiosity about crashes into a game the two of you can play.

• Stack several tall, lightweight plastic bottles, cups, or empty cans. Show your child how to throw a beanbag animal to knock them down. (It will be easier for him to do this from a seated position.) Then take turns tossing the beanbags.

• Vary the activity by using different-size balls instead of beanbags. Also try seating your child at varying distances from the stack. He'll soon discover that he needs to throw with more force when he's farther away from his target.

• Once your baby bowler improves his game, ask him to toss the beanbags while standing. Then encourage him to collect the "pins" he has blasted into all corners of the room!

GOOD THROW! It may not be fun for the hippo beanbag, but your little champ will be bowled over by this game of knock 'em down.

## RESEARCH REPORT

**In their book** *Magic Trees of the Mind,* neuroanatomist Marian Diamond and science reporter Janet Hopson stress the importance of spatial exercises, such as this beanbag bowling activity, which help spur both physical and mental development. Spatial intelligence (which includes the ability to judge distance and dimensions), they point out, "is one of the most tangible, practical mental abilities," while spatial exercises are "one of the many ways for a child to have fun and . . . let the future in."

167

THE FUN REALLY FLOWS
when you give your tot the
tools to make a little rain.

# WATERWORKS

**HE LOVES A GOOD RAINSTORM,** and she loves playing in the bath. Now she can create rain in her own tub while learning something about the properties of nature.

• Create "rainmaking" toys by making holes in the lids (or bottoms) of plastic containers. You can also use a strainer, a watering can, or a plastic sugar shaker.

• Show your toddler how to submerge the containers to fill them with water and then how to empty them. Pouring the water into a colander makes an even bigger shower. Also try gently sprinkling "raindrops" all over her head and body while singing, "Rain, rain go away, come again another day. . . ." Some toddlers will giggle with glee; others may need to wait a few months before they enjoy getting "rained" on.

• Try misting your child with water in a spray bottle (she'll likely try to mist you, too). Or show her how to use a turkey baster and let her squeeze the water into her rainmaking tools.

• An older toddler might like experimenting with a little water dripping from the showerhead—with careful monitoring of the temperature, of course. To make this activity even more enjoyable, climb into the tub with your child and let it pour!

## SKILL SPOTLIGHT

**Water play** of any kind can be a wonderful way for parents to engage their toddler's senses. This particular activity provides tactile, visual, and auditory stimulation, as the toddler feels, sees, and hears a stream of water turn into "rain." It also introduces the concepts of empty and full—and helps children understand that water can take many forms and shapes.

✔ **Concept Development**

✔ **Language Development**

✔ **Sensory Exploration**

✔ **Tactile Stimulation**

169

# WHO ARE WE?

## PLAYING DRESS-UP

**Most two-year-olds** have strong preferences when it comes to their clothing. And many are determined to dress themselves no matter how long it takes. This activity gives them the license to choose their clothes—and the luxury of dressing themselves at their leisure. Role-playing activities also act as dress rehearsals for social interactions later in life.

| | |
|---|---|
| **Creative Expression** | ✔ |
| **Imagination** | ✔ |
| **Role-Playing** | ✔ |
| **Social Skills** | ✔ |

**S**HE STARTED TOYING with your scarves, hats, and soft sweaters when she first learned to grab; she headed for your closets as soon as she could crawl. Now it's time to let her go wild with her own wardrobe. Keep a variety of dress-up items on hand (garage sales and thrift stores are great—often inexpensive—sources) and let your child don what she may to be whoever she pleases. Participate in the fun by asking her who she is that day, and invite some of her pals to join in on the act.

CHILDREN LOVE the costume dramas that dressing up inspires. A princess, a cowboy, and a movie star complete this cast.

If your child enjoys this activity, also try **Animal Actors,** page 252.

# THE MANY FORMS OF PLAY

**THIS BOOK EMPHASIZES** the playful interactions between a parent and child, but it's also important to understand how a toddler will play with peers.

One-year-olds are primarily involved in solitary play; they are busy exploring a world that is totally new to them. They are curious about other children, however, and often will imitate their actions or the noises they make.

As they get a little older, toddlers begin engaging in parallel play—that is, two or more youngsters playing with similar toys or activities side by side but without much interaction, such as building block towers individually. Around age two, as child psychologist Penelope Leach notes in *Your Baby and Child,* "Toddlers increasingly need the companionship of other children." Most adore taking part in play groups, but their ability to share toys or to indulge in mannerly back-and-forth exchanges is still a little precarious.

As they approach their third birthday, true cooperative play begins to emerge—two toddlers will build a single block tower together, for example—although there are still likely to be standoffs between toddlers over taking turns with treasured playthings or sharing the attention of beloved adults.

These early play encounters plant the seeds for acquiring important attributes such as empathy, self-control, sharing, fairness, and self-esteem, and they help cultivate much-needed tools for dealing with different social situations. As Dr. Benjamin Spock explained in *Baby and Child Care,* "In play, children . . . learn how to get along with other children and adults of different personalities, how to enjoy give-and-take, how to solve conflicts." These are valuable lessons indeed, and ones that parents can help foster by providing plenty of opportunities for their kids to play with other children. ■

# FOOTSTEP FUN

## SKILLSPOTLIGHT

**Following a trail** of any sort requires good balance and coordination. Changing the shape of the path or the distance between the squares, or asking your toddler to jump on and off the path, further challenges that balancing act. Calling out "red," "blue," and "green" as he steps on those colors also helps him expand his vocabulary.

| | |
|---|---|
| **Balance** | ✔ |
| **Coordination** | ✔ |
| **Eye-Foot Coordination** | ✔ |
| **Gross Motor Skills** | ✔ |

**E**VER SINCE YOUR TODDLER was a baby, he's been fascinated by his own feet, whether it's the feel of his toes or the look of his first walking shoes. Let him get a whole new view of his feet—as well as strong motor skills practice—by teaching him to follow his own footsteps. Trace the outline of the soles of his shoes onto colored pieces of paper. Cut out the foot shapes and glue them onto cardboard squares. Place the squares on the floor to form a path, then encourage your trailblazer to place his feet inside each of the silhouettes.

If your child enjoys this activity, also try **Balancing Act,** page 146.

By asking your little one to follow a path of colorful footprints, you provide stepping-stones to greater coordination.

# BATH TIME FOR BABY

## LESSONS IN TENDER, LOVING CARE

**Two-year-olds** are old enough to play "pretend" and to want some measure of control over their world. This activity lets your child be the parent to her "baby" and also allows her to be the little boss—a great way to practice her social skills and exercise her imagination. Learning to hold a soapy doll and wash its tiny body parts also promotes the development of fine motor skills.

| | |
|---|---|
| **Body Awareness** | ✔ |
| **Fine Motor Skills** | ✔ |
| **Imagination** | ✔ |
| **Role-Playing** | ✔ |
| **Social Skills** | ✔ |

**Y**OUR LITTLE ONE may already be playing "Mommy" or "Daddy" with her dolls and stuffed animals by rocking them, feeding them, and putting them to bed (see Doll Talk, page 196). She'll love giving her baby dolls baths, too; it's a chance for her to be the caretaker at bath time, to learn about keeping the body clean, and to shower her little friends with lots of love.

• Set up a doll's bathtub by filling a basin—or a baby bathtub if you still have one—with warm, soapy water. Provide towels, washcloths, soap, and bath toys to make it even more realistic.

• Encourage your toddler to test the water's temperature before putting her doll in ("Is it too hot for your doll? Is it too cold?") and to be gentle while washing the doll.

• Point out many of the doll's body parts ("That's her nose! And those are her toes!"). This gives your toddler more practice in labeling her own body parts, a favorite activity at this age.

• Pretend the doll is dirty and encourage her to clean specific areas such as behind the doll's ears and between the toes.

• When the doll is clean, let your toddler dry it with a towel. Then remind her to clean one more thing: her dolly's teeth!

SCRUB-A-DUB-DUB, it's dolly in the tub! Your two-year-old will love being in charge of her baby's sudsy sponge bath.

## RESEARCH REPORT

**A few short months ago,** your toddler wasn't able to engage in this type of imaginative play. Kurt Fischer, a Harvard cognitive neuroscientist and educator, has tracked the cranial growth, brain-wave activity, and density of neural connections in children to show that the brain is subject to a series of growth spurts at certain predictable interludes. One such spurt occurs between eighteen and twenty-four months, he says, endowing a child with a capacity for symbolic representation. In other words, for the first time, your child can make the mental leap that an inanimate object (such as her doll) is a "baby" in need of a good washing.

177

# CARE FOR THE ANIMALS

## LEARNING TO NURTURE OTHER CREATURES

**This game of "pretend"** teaches your child empathy and lets her practice nurturing others. It also helps build her vocabulary: birds have wings, tigers have paws, and elephants have trunks. And talking to your toddler about the ways animals can get sick ("The horsie ate too much sugar and got a tummy ache") expands her knowledge of animal life.

| | |
|---|---|
| **Concept Development** | ✔ |
| **Creative Expression** | ✔ |
| **Fine Motor Skills** | ✔ |
| **Imagination** | ✔ |
| **Role-Playing** | ✔ |

**S**HE LOVES HER ANIMALS (both the real and the stuffed ones) and she's keen on bandages and the notions of "boo-boo" and "sick." That means she's more than ready to open up a veterinary practice in her own home. It's all pretend, of course, but she'll enjoy learning how to care for her little friends.

• Help your toddler gather her favorite stuffed and plastic animals. (Make sure they are more than 1¾ inches, or 4.5 cm, in diameter so they won't pose a choking hazard.)

• Provide small boxes or berry baskets for her to use as cages or carriers. She can use napkins or small scarves as blankets.

• Talk to her about the different ways in which animals can get hurt: how they can cut their paws, get bugs in their ears, break their wings, or get stomachaches.

• Help her care for her sick animals by washing and bandaging their wounds, wrapping their broken limbs with gauze, and giving them a clean, quiet place to sleep (plus lots of pats and kind words). A toy doctor's kit will provide helpful instruments for examining and treating her ailing friends, too.

HELPING HER PLAY pretend vet is a natural way to nurture her knowledge of all living things.

179

# MAGIC CUPS

## A CHALLENGING MEMORY GAME

### SKILLSPOTLIGHT

**When your toddler** was a baby, you could cover up a toy and she would forget it ever existed. Now she understands that the covered object is still there—this is called object permanence—and she's delighted to find it. By asking her to concentrate on one cup as it moves, you encourage her to recall the toy and you help sharpen her visual memory.

| | |
|---|---|
| **Problem Solving** | ✓ |
| **Visual Memory** | ✓ |

**T**HIS TODDLER ACTIVITY is a step up from peekaboo, but operates on the same principle. First it's here, then it's gone, then it's back again—but only if your toddler remembers where it was! To start the game, hide a small toy under one of three cups while your child is watching. Then slowly move the cups around and ask her to guess which one conceals the toy.

• If you've seen street entertainers play this game, you know it can be confusing, even for adults. So don't move the cups too quickly or else she won't be able to keep track of her toy.

WHICH CUP hides the yellow ducky? She'll love trying to keep tabs—especially if you applaud her when she's right.

181

# BEEP, BEEP

PLAYING WITH TRUCKS AND CARS

**Playing with toy cars** is a great way for your toddler to exercise her imagination, and it gives her a chance to imitate a mundane part of your adult world: driving the car. (Don't worry; it's interesting to her!) It also lets her develop the fine motor skills of pushing and pulling and teaches her to discern noises in her everyday world.

| | |
|---|---|
| **Creative Expression** | ✔ |
| **Fine Motor Skills** | ✔ |
| **Imagination** | ✔ |
| **Language Development** | ✔ |

**M**OST TWO-YEAR-OLDS are fascinated with all things vehicular, ranging from their own strollers to the cars, trucks, and buses on the street to the choo-choo trains they see in picture books. Toddlers are especially excited by watching trains and cars enter tunnels and cross bridges. Enhance their wonder (and let them feel like they're finally behind the wheel of one of these grown-up contraptions) by giving them a chance to play with toy trucks, cars, and tunnels.

• Choose a large, colorful toy vehicle, rather than a miniature one, so she can control it more easily.

• Show her how to push a truck along the floor. Teach her noises a truck makes— the "beep, beep" of the horn, the "scre-e-e-ch" of the tires, and the "vrooom" of the engine. Point out these sounds to her when you're driving in a real car.

STEER HER ENERGY into a little creative car play, and watch those motor skills grow.

• Cut holes in both ends of a big cardboard box to make a tunnel and show her how to push the truck through it. Talk about the parts of the truck (steering wheel, tires) and explain why she might need to "turn on" the headlights when she drives into the dark tunnel. Also see if she can guess which part of the truck will come out of the tunnel first— the front or the back.

## RESEARCH REPORT

**A toddler's** apparently boundless enthusiasm for play reflects the fact that she is in a unique and wondrous period of development. A child's brain at age two years consumes twice as much metabolic energy as an adult's, and it also possesses twice as many synapses (the connections between nerve cells that convey the electrical impulses needed for all the body's functions, including cognition). "Children are biologically primed for learning during this time," state neurologist Ann Barnet and her coauthor and husband, Richard, in their book *The Youngest Minds*. This golden window of opportunity lasts only until around age ten, when the brain starts to lose the synaptic connections that have not yet been put to use.

# DRIVE THE FIRE TRUCK

**Drive the Fire Truck**

*to the* **tune** *of* **"Ten Little Indians"**

**Hurry, hurry, drive the fire truck,**
*make driving motions*

**hurry, hurry, drive the fire truck,
hurry, hurry, drive the fire truck,
ding, ding, ding, ding, ding!**
*swing hand as if ringing a bell*

**Hurry, hurry, climb the ladder,**
*pretend to climb a ladder*

**hurry, hurry, climb the ladder,
hurry, hurry, climb the ladder,
ding, ding, ding, ding, ding!**

**Hurry, hurry, squirt the water,**
*make squirting motions*

**hurry, hurry, squirt the water,
hurry, hurry, squirt the water,
ding, ding, ding, ding, ding!**

**Language Development** ✔

**Role-Playing** ✔

 **ING THE BELL!** Sound the alarm! This fast-paced song lets your truck-loving tyke pretend to drive the biggest, brightest rig around—a fire truck—while letting him play one of the most exciting roles in town. Sing "Drive the Fire Truck" (lyrics at left) and face your child while you teach him the hand gestures, or have him stand with his back to you and help him do the gestures himself. If he is ready to act out the role of a firefighter, find a heavy-duty cardboard box, paint it bright red, and push him around in it as you sing the song and he makes the motions.

If your child enjoys this activity, also try **Train Trips,** page 150.

YOUR LITTLE FIRE CHIEF will think this is the hottest game of all when he realizes he gets to drive the truck.

185

# PURSE TREASURES

**G**RANTED, a toddler's boundless curiosity about the treasures in your purse or briefcase is adorable. But it can lead to chaos (lost credit cards, for example) and even danger (from items such as opened pill-boxes and pointy pencils). Safely encourage her explorations by giving her a purse of her very own. Fill it with harmless objects such as those she might find in your bag: a comb, keys, a mirror, a notepad—even a wallet. Encourage her to find things without looking ("Can you feel the keys in there?"), or ask her to name each item as she pulls it out.

IT LOOKS LIKE she's just playing grown-up. But her very own bag—filled with safe items—lets her explore different objects and learn about their uses.

## SKILLSPOTLIGHT

**You can enrich** your child's understanding of all the items in her purse by explaining the use of each object as she pulls it out. ("I'm glad you found the car keys. Now we can drive to the grocery store.") Frequently changing the objects in the purse further challenges her identifying skills.

✔ **Concept Development**

✔ **Language Development**

✔ **Listening Skills**

✔ **Tactile Discrimination**

# TOUCH AND TELL

## SKILL SPOTLIGHT

**Learning to describe** the objects in his world helps your child feel some measure of control over them. It also helps him develop his language skills. And adding a tactile component to his developing visual memory helps him understand objects in a three-dimensional way.

| | |
|---|---|
| **Concept Development** | ✔ |
| **Language Development** | ✔ |
| **Listening Skills** | ✔ |
| **Problem Solving** | ✔ |
| **Tactile Discrimination** | ✔ |

**YOUR TODDLER** is getting into just about everything now, mostly because he's compelled to explore how everything feels, tastes, sounds, looks, and moves. Help your young sleuth investigate and identify the sensations of different shapes and textures with this variation of the classic show-and-tell game.

• Place a familiar object such as his toy truck, ball, doll, or favorite spoon or cup inside a pillowcase or canvas bag.

• Ask your child to reach into the pillowcase (no peeking!) and feel the object. Then ask him to guess what it is. (He may need to guess more than once.) If he doesn't guess the right answer, tell him what it is before he grows too frustrated.

• Pull out the object and talk about its tactile characteristics. Introduce the concepts of hard and soft, fuzzy and smooth.

• Repeat the exercise with another toy. Encourage him to use the words you've introduced as he's guessing what the toy is.

• To vary the game, let him hide a toy in the pillowcase so that you can play detective. Or put an object inside the pillowcase and ask him to guess what it is by feeling it from the outside.

HE'LL GET A FEEL FOR TEXTURES and learn to name those sensations in this hands-on guessing game.

189

# PLAY WITH CLAY

## MAKING SHAPES AND SCULPTURES

**Playing with modeling clay** allows your child to experience shapes and textures in three dimensions. And manipulating the clay builds fine motor skills and stimulates the senses. Help expand your child's vocabulary by teaching her words for colors, shapes, and textures.

**MAKING YOUR OWN**

Mix 1 cup flour, 1 cup salt, 1 tablespoon cream of tartar, 1 cup water, and 1 tablespoon vegetable oil. Simmer in a pot until clay begins to pull away from the pot's sides. When cool, add 5 drops of food coloring, and knead until smooth.

| | |
|---|---|
| **Cause and Effect** | ✔ |
| **Creative Expression** | ✔ |
| **Fine Motor Skills** | ✔ |
| **Language Development** | ✔ |
| **Sensory Exploration** | ✔ |

**Y**OU MAY HAVE FOND MEMORIES of molding clay into silly shapes, and now your two-year-old is ready to dive into the colorful stuff. Purchase nontoxic modeling clay in any toy store or make a few colorful batches yourself (see the recipe for clay at left). Provide ample working space and a few safe tools, such as a rolling pin, a potato masher, and cookie cutters.

• Most young children prefer to experiment with mushing the clay into abstract shapes. Guide her in manipulating the clay by rolling it into a ball and letting her smash it. Or make a long roll that she can tear into pieces and press back together.

• Show your child how simple shapes such as circles, squares, and triangles fit together to make recognizable objects such as faces, hats, or trees.

• To store the clay, gather several airtight containers and mark each lid with the same color as the clay it contains. When she's done playing with the clay, ask her to put it away in its appropriate container.

TURN HER LOOSE with some tools and colorful clay, and watch her creativity take shape.

## RESEARCH REPORT

**Squishing and shaping** modeling clay does more than encourage the budding artist in your child. By allowing her to handle these and other tactile delights, you're helping her develop "knowledge of how the world works and proficiency at using different materials," states Esther Thelen, a psychologist at Indiana University in Bloomington. Educational psychologist Jane Healy is another believer in the benefits of clay, sand, finger paint, and mud, which she says help refine a child's tactile ability. Healy also offers this advice to fastidious parents: "If you tend to be fanatic about cleanliness, close your eyes and imagine little [neural] dendrites branching inside that muddy head."

191

# IF THE SHOE FITS

## SKILL SPOTLIGHT

**This easy-to-assemble project** allows toddlers to practice their early sorting skills and make discoveries about size and materials. As you talk together, your toddler's use of language expands; when you ask him to guess or make assumptions about the different shoes and their uses, you encourage the development of his problem-solving abilities.

| | |
|---|---|
| **Classifying Skills** | ✔ |
| **Language Development** | ✔ |

ANY CLASSIFYING ACTIVITIES are too frustrating for younger toddlers, but by age two to two-and-a-half, most children are eager to perform a fairly simple sorting task—especially if it involves playing with Mommy's or Daddy's shoes. Put two or three pairs of shoes on a table, separating each shoe from its mate. Choose shoes of distinct sizes and types, such as adult boots, baby shoes, and your fuzzy slippers. Ask your child which shoes match. As he searches for the mate, talk about the types of shoes, whom they fit, and what they're used for. Some toddlers find it easier to sort if they have shoe boxes to put the pairs into.

If your child enjoys this activity, also try **Color Clusters,** page 198.

WHICH SHOES BELONG TOGETHER?
Toddlers can try to successfully combine
pairs of family footwear in a challenging
game of mix-and-match.

# MYSTERY SOUNDS

## SKILL SPOTLIGHT

**Young children love** guessing games, and this one helps fine-tune auditory skills. Locating an object by listening to a sound teaches your toddler to find an answer through the process of elimination—and it reinforces the notion that a thoughtful guess is part of the learning process.

| | |
|---|---|
| **Listening Skills** | ✔ |
| **Problem Solving** | ✔ |

**WHAT'S THAT SOUND?** Where is it coming from? Those are the questions to pose to young detectives in this game of auditory hide-and-seek. Use a long-playing musical toy or other noisemaking item (such as a kitchen timer, clock, or metronome) and hide it on a low shelf or table—or behind a cupboard door. Search together with your child to locate the source of the sound and retrieve the object. As you hunt, ask your toddler to try to guess what toy or object is making the mysterious sound.

If your child enjoys this activity, also try **Mighty Megaphones,** page 236.

USING HER EARS to find
the source of a sound may
become a young sleuth's
favorite guessing game.

# DOLL TALK

**S**EEING A TODDLER'S TENDERNESS toward dolls, teddies, and other cuddlies is touching. Her enthusiasm, however, may sometimes make her a bit too rough—especially with animals or other children. You can help refine her nurturing abilities by interacting with your child as she plays with her pretend friends.

• Give your child a doll or stuffed animal to hold. Suggest that she gently brush the doll's hair or rock it in her arms. Or help her learn to pat animals by showing her how.

• Tell her that the doll or teddy bear is cold, and ask her to comfort it by putting shoes and socks and warm clothes on the doll (she may need help with snaps and buttons) or by covering the plush toy with a blanket.

• Then suggest that she feed her doll or pet because it hasn't eaten all day and must be quite hungry. She can offer it pretend food, or give her a spoon and a small dish of cereal or raisins, which are easy to clean up.

• Join your child in singing a lullaby to her charge while helping her rock it to sleep, then ask her to gently tuck it into bed.

If your child enjoys this activity, also try **Bath Time for Baby,** page 176.

WHEN DADDY SHOWS his daughter how to care for her doll, he provides an important lesson in nurturing others.

**RESEARCH**REPORT

**While many adults struggle** with the finer points of grammar, we might be humbled to learn that 90 percent of the sentences spoken by the average three-year-old are grammatically correct. The mistakes they make usually result from an overly zealous application of the rules. In English, for example, we usually indicate plurals by adding an "s" or "es" to the end of a noun (rivers, churches, and buses, for instance) and use the suffix "ed" to convey the past tense of a verb (patted, changed, and kissed, to name a few). So why do we laugh at a toddler who says, "I see three mouses" or "You gived me a doll"? Hey, she's just following the rules!

197

# COLOR CLUSTERS

## SKILL SPOTLIGHT

**This elementary abacus** enhances your toddler's ability to categorize objects by helping him identify different colors and sizes. It also provides a great opportunity to introduce your child to comparison words, such as big, bigger, and biggest.

| | |
|---|---|
| **Classifying Skills** | ✓ |
| **Concept Development** | ✓ |
| **Coordination** | ✓ |
| **Language Development** | ✓ |

OLORFUL, REVOLVING BALLS on a rope are sure to catch toddlers' eyes, as they love both bright colors and spinning motions. But besides being fun, this activity can teach your little one some pretty big concepts. To start, thread a thin rope through a group of colored balls with holes (available at many toy stores) and tie the rope firmly between two chairs. Show your toddler how to spin the balls and slide them from one end of the rope to the other. Then ask him to spin only a large ball or only a particular color.

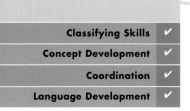

If your child enjoys this activity, also try **Water Targets,** page 202.

198

MAKING THE BRIGHT BALLS SPIN quickly is fun, but so is learning to identify blue and red, large and small, and more and less.

199

30 MONTHS AND UP

2¹⁄₂

# WATER TARGETS

## MAKING A SPLASH LANDING

**SKILL**SPOTLIGHT

**This water game** helps build your toddler's eye-hand coordination and gross motor skills. The activity is also a fun way to introduce your toddler to counting ("That's one in, two in, three in. Look! Three balls in the water!").

| | |
|---|---|
| **Coordination** | ✔ |
| **Counting Concepts** | ✔ |
| **Eye-Hand Coordination** | ✔ |
| **Gross Motor Skills** | ✔ |

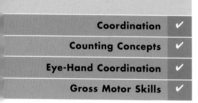ATER, BALLS, THROWING, SPLASHING— the elements in this activity may get you and your toddler a bit wet, but she'll enjoy it so much you won't mind. Find two or three big plastic bowls or pots and fill them halfway with water. Gather an assortment of small balls, preferably ones that float (plastic or tennis balls work well). Ask your child to throw the balls into the water targets. Count how many balls she can land inside each bowl and be sure to applaud every attempt, even when she misses. As she gets better at this activity, increase the challenge by having her stand farther away from the water-filled bowls.

If your child enjoys this activity, also try **Up It Goes!,** page 212.

YOUR LITTLE PITCHER makes a big splash when she gets the ball in—and she fine-tunes her coordination as she aims for her water targets.

203

# PAINT PRIMER

## SKILL SPOTLIGHT

**At thirty months,** he's only just beginning to realize that he can create something, whether it's a scribble with a crayon or a painting covered with brushstrokes. Letting him paint what he wants helps him feel confident about expressing himself visually. Turning everyday objects into artistic tools develops your toddler's creativity as well as his fine motor control and eye-hand coordination.

| | |
|---|---|
| **Creative Expression** | ✔ |
| **Eye-Hand Coordination** | ✔ |
| **Fine Motor Skills** | ✔ |
| **Tactile Stimulation** | ✔ |

**H**E'S NOT OLD ENOUGH to paint still lifes, and you may not recognize much of what he creates, but every toddler has an inner artist that's itching to get out. Help set that creative spirit free by providing paints and tools that even the smallest hands can handle.

• Set out several colors of nontoxic (such as tempera) paints in small bowls. Collect a variety of painting tools, too, such as paintbrushes, dish scrubbers, and sponges cut into shapes.

• Show your child how to dip his utensils into the paint and to roll or brush them on the paper. Then let him experiment with colors and designs. Remember, there's no right or wrong way at this age—so let him make whatever inspires him.

• If your child seems to want some guidance from you, paint a few large shapes (circles, squares, triangles) and let him color them—but do not expect him to stay inside the lines.

• Don't forgo the fun because you're afraid of muss and fuss: tape large sheets of paper onto an easily washable surface (such as the kitchen floor or table) and plop your junior Picasso in the bath when he's done.

If your child enjoys this activity, also try **Colorful Collages,** page 222.

"LOOK WHAT I MADE, DADDY! It's a fire truck!" Broadening your child's creative palette is as easy as putting paint to paper.

# FLASHLIGHT FUN

## SKILLSPOTLIGHT

**Searching for an object** presents a problem that your child has to concentrate on in order to solve. The first step, of course, is to listen to your description of the hidden object, which involves comprehension skills. Then she has to think about places that aren't immediately visible to her—a type of abstract thinking that is a big step for a young child. This nighttime game may also allay fears and negative feelings that children often have about darkness.

| | |
|---|---|
| **Listening Skills** | ✔ |
| **Problem Solving** | ✔ |
| **Social Skills** | ✔ |
| **Visual Memory** | ✔ |

**IELDING A FLASHLIGHT** sparks wonder in most toddlers: the tool gives them control over the dark and changes how everything looks.

• Start this activity in the evening by hiding one of your child's favorite items, such as a doll, a book, or her beloved teddy bear. Limit the hunting area to one or two rooms so it won't be too difficult for her to find the hidden treasure.

• Tell your toddler what to look for, then turn off (or just dim) the lights, and hand her a lightweight flashlight. (You may have to show her how to use it at first.) Equip yourself with a flashlight, too, so you can join her.

• Keep the game lively and silly by providing her with clues: "You're getting warmer, warmer, warmer! Oops! Now you're cooling down." If she gets frustrated, use the beam of your flashlight to help guide her to the hiding place.

• This is an ideal activity for a toddler to play with an older sibling or a group of kids, because you can hide several objects at one time—some in harder places than others—and it's a great spectacle to watch the children waving their bright beams of light at one another.

A TREASURE HUNT becomes
even more exciting—and
challenging—for your child
when she has a flashlight
to use in the dark.

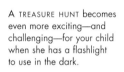

# NATURE VS. NURTURE

**DO WE COME** into this world imprinted with immutable abilities, foibles, and personality traits? Or are we born blank slates, waiting for the environment to etch its effect on our psyches? For many scientists, brain research has settled the age-old question of nature versus nurture once and for all. The resounding verdict? It's a draw.

For decades, behavioral studies have suggested that some traits, such as aggressiveness, shyness, and a willingness to take risks, have a genetic origin. But just when Mother Nature seemed to be the winner in the ancient debate, neurologists demonstrated how unfinished the human brain is at birth and how environmental factors exert powerful influences on a person's disposition—even altering the shape of the brain in some cases. Scientists have reconciled these two competing forces by concluding that while people are indeed born with certain tendencies and abilities, the degree to which those traits are manifested depends a great deal on what they're exposed to, especially during early childhood. As neurologist Ann Barnet states in her book *The Youngest Minds,* "Current estimates made by behavioral geneticists for the relative influence of heritable factors and environment are about 50–50."

This split has important implications for parents. For one thing, it means that if a child is innately inclined to some particular behavior, parents can work with her to overcome that tendency—helping her become more outgoing if she's shy, for example, or instilling a little impulse control if she's inclined to take too many risks. Conversely, this split also suggests that even if a child is born with certain gifts, such as outstanding musical or artistic ability, those talents might never be realized if there's no opportunity for them to flourish. ∎

# HEY MR. JUMPING JACK

**Hey Mr. Jumping Jack**

**Hey Mr. Jumping Jack,**
**a funny old man,**
**he jumps and he jumps**
**whenever he can.**
**He jumps way up high,**
**he jumps way down low,**
**and he jumps and he jumps**
**wherever he goes.**

**Come on and jump!**

**Hey Mr. Jumping Jack,**
**a funny old man,**
**he wiggles and he wiggles**
**whenever he can.**
**He wiggles way up high,**
**he wiggles way down low,**
**and he wiggles and he wiggles**
**wherever he goes.**

**Come on and wiggle!**

 **G** ET YOUR LITTLE ONE giggling and wiggling to this upbeat chant that encourages rhythm and movement. Hold your child on your lap, facing you, and then tap out a rhythm with your feet as you say the words. When Mr. Jumping Jack jumps high, lift your toddler up high; when he jumps low, give him just a little lift. For the second verse, wiggle your child gently as you lift him high and low (hard shaking is dangerous). Add your own verses and movements such as clapping, flapping, jumping, and waving. And when your toddler is steady on his feet, let him jump and wiggle on his own as you chant and clap.

| | |
|---|---|
| **Listening Skills** | ✓ |
| **Rhythm Exploration** | ✓ |

If your child enjoys this activity, also try **Teddy Bear Tunes,** page 218.

SECURE IN MOMMY'S ARMS, your toddler will laugh out loud as he soars up and down to the words of this cheery chant.

# UP IT GOES!

## SKILL SPOTLIGHT

**This game challenges** your toddler's coordination and visual acuity. To toss the ball straight up, she has to try to raise the blanket in sync with you. To catch it squarely on the blanket, she needs to keep her eye on the ball as it comes back down. This activity takes planning and some sense of cooperation with her partner—and she may need to practice it several times before she catches on.

| | |
|---|---|
| **Cause and Effect** | ✔ |
| **Eye-Foot Coordination** | ✔ |
| **Eye-Hand Coordination** | ✔ |

**S**UMMER OR WINTER, indoors or out, a beach ball—or another very lightweight ball—makes for all kinds of merriment when there's a toddler around. To play this game, you and your child hold opposite ends of a blanket or mini-parachute. Place a beach ball in the center and toss it up in the air, trying to catch it in the parachute as it comes down again. Start with gentle tosses so the ball doesn't go too high. As your toddler's coordination improves, bounce the ball higher.

SHE FOLLOWS THE BOUNCING ball in this delightful game that exercises her ability to coordinate muscle movements with motion.

213

30 MONTHS 2½ AND UP

PUTTING TWO AND TWO TOGETHER to make a butterfly is just the kind of puzzle a toddler is ready to tackle.

# PAPER PUZZLE

FITTING THE BIG PIECES TOGETHER

**I**F YOUR CHILD is already happily playing with wooden puzzles and shape sorters, it might be a prime time to enhance his ability to understand and organize shapes spatially by creating an elementary puzzle for him. Find an engaging, colorful picture of something your toddler might like—an animal, a truck, a baby, or a favorite food, for instance. (Magazines are rich sources for large photographs.) Then glue the image onto a letter-size piece of paper or cardboard. Cut the picture into four large sections. Now help him rearrange the pieces to put the picture back together again. When he's figured that out, you can make the puzzle more difficult by cutting it into smaller pieces.

If your child enjoys this activity, also try **Shape Sorter**, page 244.

## SKILL SPOTLIGHT

**This activity allows** your toddler to exercise his understanding of spatial relations. It also lets him create—and re-create—a picture that he likes (a test of his visual memory skills), which will give him the confidence to eventually try more difficult puzzles.

✔ **Concept Development**

✔ **Problem Solving**

✔ **Size and Shape Discrimination**

✔ **Visual Discrimination**

✔ **Visual Memory**

# COMMON SCENTS

## **SKILL**SPOTLIGHT

**Here's an activity** that lets your child further explore the many aspects of her sensory world. Bringing the realm of scents to her attention helps her become more aware of the hundreds of different odors—pleasant and pungent—around us. Teaching her the words for different smells, and the objects from which they emanate, also expands her vocabulary.

| | |
|---|---|
| **Language Development** | ✔ |
| **Problem Solving** | ✔ |
| **Sensory Exploration** | ✔ |
| **Visual Memory** | ✔ |

 **HE SMILES WHEN EATING** a cookie and purses her little lips at the sight of broccoli, so you know she has a discriminating palate. But how's her sense of smell? Help her learn to match aroma to food with this simple sniffing game.

• Gather several strongly scented foods that your child already knows, such as chocolate-chip cookies, oranges, and onions.

• Blindfold her with a scarf (or just cover her eyes with your hand). Then ask her to take a big sniff (no peeking!) and guess what the smells are. After she guesses, let her taste the food to better match different smells with different tastes.

• As she masters this activity, choose foods with subtler aromas. For example, see if she can distinguish between a peach and an apple or a lemon and an orange.

• Try outside smells, too. Test her olfactory memory on flowers, pine needles, damp dirt, and common herbs.

• Ask your toddler to identify smells she might encounter in the neighborhood, such as bread in a bakery or barbecued chicken in a restaurant.

PHEW! The pungent smell of raw onion is easy to recognize, but how about those orange slices?

# TEDDY BEAR TUNES

**T**ODDLERS LOVE TEDDY BEARS— and the rhythm and repetition of these teddy tunes give them a timeless appeal. With your child on your knee, bounce her gently to the beat of these songs while encouraging her to sing along—or join her (and her plush toys) in acting out the appropriate gestures to accompany the lyrics.

## THE BEAR

*to the tune of* "For He's a Jolly Good Fellow"

The bear went over the mountain,
the bear went over the mountain,
the bear went over the mountain,
to see what she could see.

To see what she could see,
To see what she could see.

The bear went over the mountain,
the bear went over the mountain,
the bear went over the mountain,
to see what she could see.

## TEDDY BEAR, TEDDY BEAR

**Teddy bear, teddy bear, turn around.**
*turn around in circles with your child while you chant*

**Teddy bear, teddy bear,
touch the ground.**
*touch the floor*

**Teddy bear, teddy bear,
show your shoe.**
*bring one foot forward*

**Teddy bear, teddy bear,
crawl right through.**
*let your child crawl between your legs*

**Oh when the bears
go marching in,
oh when the bears go marching in,
oh, how I want to be a big teddy,
when the bears go marching in.**
*march in place with your child*

**Oh when the bears
go jumping in,
oh when the bears go jumping in,
oh, how I want to be a big teddy,
when the bears go jumping in.**
*jump up and down*

**Oh when the bears
go wiggling in . . .**
*wiggle your body*

**Oh when the bears
go tiptoeing in . . .**
*tiptoe around the room*

**Oh when the bears
go hopping in . . .**
*hop up and down*

**Bears are sleeping,
bears are sleeping,
in their caves, in their caves.
Waiting for the springtime,
waiting for the springtime.
Shh! Shh! Shh!
Shh! Shh! Shh!**

DADDY'S KNEE is the
perfect place for a duet
of teddy bear songs that
will help your young cub
expand her language
and listening skills.

# ON TARGET!

## SKILL SPOTLIGHT

**The act of jumping** works muscles on both sides of the body, thereby increasing bilateral coordination. This provides a good counterpoint to activities, such as rolling a ball, that work only one side of the body. Jumping also improves eye-foot coordination and balance in an older toddler: she needs to put her feet where she's looking and then she has to try to stay upright after landing.

| | |
|---|---|
| **Balance** | ✔ |
| **Eye-Foot Coordination** | ✔ |
| **Gross Motor Skills** | ✔ |
| **Spatial Awareness** | ✔ |

**J**UMPING IS a big accomplishment for toddlers, one that takes coordination, strength, and a dash of courage. It's also a skill that thrills: just observe the joy on your puddle jumper's face after leaping into a big pool of rainwater. You can help improve her aim and boost her confidence by setting up jumping target practice using a stable stool, block, or another safe launching pad that won't slide out from beneath her.

• Use a large piece of construction paper or a colored paper plate as a target, and adhere it to the ground with strong packaging tape so it won't slip when she lands. Encourage your child to jump directly onto the target—this will likely take some practice. Applaud her every attempt.

• As your toddler's abilities increase, make the target smaller. Or ask her to jump from a greater (though still safe) height.

• Some children may be nervous about bounding into space this way. Soothe her fears by showing her how to jump— or hold her hand as she makes the leap the first few times. Once she becomes confident in her jumping abilities, she'll want to aim for the target again and again.

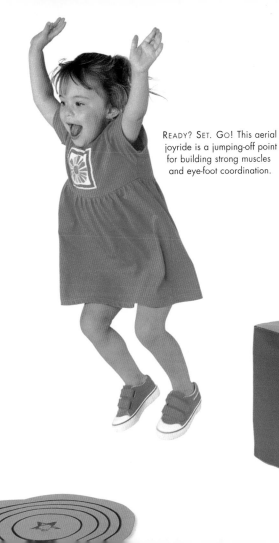

READY? SET. GO! This aerial joyride is a jumping-off point for building strong muscles and eye-foot coordination.

221

# COLORFUL COLLAGES

## COLLECTING INTRIGUING IMAGES

**Letting your child select** his own pictures for a collage gives him a chance to practice expressing his preferences. Encouraging him to discuss the images is a way to help build his vocabulary. Teaching him to handle glue and sticky pieces of paper also aids him in developing his fine motor skills.

| | |
|---|---|
| **Creative Expression** | ✔ |
| **Fine Motor Skills** | ✔ |
| **Language Development** | ✔ |
| **Visual Discrimination** | ✔ |

**E**VEN AT THIS EARLY AGE, your child has distinct likes and dislikes. He may be fascinated by music, for instance, or animals, or occupations such as gardening and cooking. Encourage your toddler to enjoy his natural interests by helping him create a fun collage made from an assortment of related pictures.

• Collect colorful pictures of his passion from magazines, newspapers, or even junk mail, and place them in a bowl.

• Invite your toddler to look through them and talk about the pictures as he picks them up. Ask him to name the objects he sees (for example, a violin, a whale, or a flower).

• Ask him to pick out his favorite pictures. Place them on a large sheet of heavyweight paper, such as construction paper.

• Using nontoxic glue, show him how to put glue on the back of a picture and press it onto the paper to make a collage.

• Once you both have completed the collage, hang it someplace visible, such as in his bedroom, on the refrigerator, or even in the front hallway. Children's art should be seen—not hidden!

"I LIKE DOLPHINS because they live in the ocean." Learn more about your child while creating a work of art that reflects his personality and preferences.

## RESEARCH REPORT

**Enriching experiences** such as assembling a collage provide children with creative stimulation that is vital to their development. Researchers at Baylor College of Medicine in Houston, Texas, found that children deprived of playthings and playmates (as well as nurturing caregivers) have brains 20 to 30 percent smaller than normal. To provide the proper stimulation, parents needn't stock up on all sorts of techno-gadgets and expensive toys; an extensive study conducted at the University of Alabama found that the basics, such as art supplies, blocks, and puzzles, were still the best at promoting cognitive and physical development.

# BEAUTIFUL BOX

## SKILL SPOTLIGHT

**This project nurtures** a toddler's creative spirit while encouraging her to express herself on something other than flat paper. By combining drawing, painting, coloring, and collage, it introduces her to several different artistic media. This activity also polishes fine motor skills and can help develop communication skills, especially if parents engage their children in a discussion as they're decorating the box together.

| Creative Expression | ✔ |
| Fine Motor Skills | ✔ |
| Social Skills | ✔ |

**D**ECORATING A BOX for her toy treasures will help take your toddler's natural (albeit elementary) artistic abilities to a new dimension. Use a plain or colored cardboard box (or cover a printed box with white paper). Give your child non-permanent markers and crayons for drawing lines and circles on the box; help her glue glitter, ribbons, or paper cutouts on it as well. Start with a theme (such as the sea) and encourage her to elaborate on that topic with stickers (fish, boats, and beach balls). When she's done, write her name on her special box.

If your child enjoys this activity, also try **Paint Primer,** page 204.

TURN HER LOOSE with crayons and stickers, and watch her create a treasure chest of her own.

# TURN AROUND

**Turn Around**

to the *tune* of **"Frère Jacques"**

**Turn around,
turn around,
touch your toes,
touch your toes.**

**Do a little jumping,
do a little jumping.**

**Squat real low.
Up we go!**

*perform the actions indicated by
the lyrics; do them slowly until
your child learns all the movements*

| | |
|---|---|
| **Balance** | ✔ |
| **Coordination** | ✔ |
| **Gross Motor Skills** | ✔ |

**T**HIS MOVE-YOUR-BODY SONG is a fun way to combine singing with some vigorous exercise. Sing "Turn Around" a few times, following the instructions in the lyrics (at left), and exaggerate your actions—for example, leap high in the air when you sing, "Up we go!" Your little jumping bean will love imitating you; at the same time he'll develop better body control and gross motor skills. Acting out the lyrics also improves your child's comprehension of the concepts of up and down and high and low.

MOVING TO THE MUSIC will help him build confidence in his body step by step.

# MINI MIMES

**SKILL**SPOTLIGHT

**Toddlers love to assist adults** and to perform all the grown-up tasks they do. These miming activities let your child delve into an imaginary world that includes an adult and adult activities—the perfect combination. Cooperating on a joint project—however imaginary—also helps her learn social skills such as sharing, offering, and expressing gratitude.

| Body Awareness | ✔ |
| Creative Expression | ✔ |
| Creative Movement | ✔ |
| Imagination | ✔ |
| Social Skills | ✔ |

 **HE WANTS TO DO** just about everything you do, right? Let her participate in grown-up activities by miming all sorts of fun things along with you.

• Try having a tea party—with no tea set. Act out pouring the tea, passing the plate of cookies, and drinking and eating. Be sure to say "Please," "Thank you," and "Mmm . . . this tea is delicious!" That helps your child learn good manners, and the conversation brings the party to life.

• Bake a cake without any pans or ingredients. Crack the pretend eggs, mix in the flour, and pour the batter into a pan. Dust the flour off your hands when you're all done—and then treat yourselves to a big piece of scrumptious cake.

• Other activities to act out include flying an airplane, cleaning up the house, or galloping around on a horse.

If your child enjoys this activity, also try **Animal Actors,** page 252.

228

IT'S JUST PRETEND TEA, but a play tea party fires up her imagination and teaches her to say "Yes, please, I would love some more" and "Thank you very much."

# TODDLER TALK

**JUST AS CHILDREN** seem to come into this world hardwired to learn language, parents instinctively do much to promote this vital skill. In countless cultures around the world, for example, parents naturally speak to their babies and toddlers in a high-pitched, repetitive, singsong voice that linguists have dubbed "parentese." It is now universally accepted that this melodic, pared-down speech speeds up a child's ability to connect words with the objects they represent and offers the simplified syntax and repetition she needs to learn many of the rules of grammar.

Parents can do several other things to help. As the Research Report on page 79 highlights, the simple act of talking to your child—a lot—even before she is capable of talking back, is critical to building her vocabulary. "Tell your baby and toddler everything you can think of," advise Dr. Marian Diamond and Janet Hopson in *Magic Trees of the Mind*. "Bathe your child with spoken language."

Having a toddler point to the pictures in a book, echo some of your words, or add sound effects keeps her engaged and helps stretch her attention span. Introducing new words in a real-life, emotional context also is important—a child picks up the meaning of "later" and "now" much more quickly when the words are linked to the time that she's going to get a favorite snack or go to the park. Feeding her boundless interest in knowing the names of everything she sees in the house, passes in the car, or spots in the local market is key to fulfilling her labeling instinct, which is going full throttle as she approaches her second birthday. Finally, keep in mind that the benefits of hands-on parenting: cuddling a child as you talk or read together adds a dimension of loving, physical contact that also seems to hasten language acquisition. ∎

# CAR CAPERS

## SKILLSPOTLIGHT

**Successfully matching colors** helps train a toddler's eye to compare and contrast different objects. It also engages his mind by making him link up two very different items that share one common characteristic (in this case, color). And repeating the names of the colors aloud as he matches the car to the paper helps strengthen his vocabulary.

| | |
|---|---|
| **Classifying Skills** | ✔ |
| **Concept Development** | ✔ |
| **Problem Solving** | ✔ |
| **Visual Discrimination** | ✔ |

 OST TWO-YEAR-OLDS are fascinated by colors and are compelled to identify them. This activity takes advantage of your child's interest in colors while strengthening his ability to recognize them.

• Find some paper that matches the colors of cars or trucks in his toy collection. Say the color of the paper as you lay it on the floor. Park a car or truck of the same color on each piece of paper (red car on red paper, yellow truck on yellow paper, for example). Then mix them up and ask your child to "drive" the vehicles onto their color-coded parking spots.

If your child enjoys this activity, also try **Shape Sorter,** page 244.

FINDING THE RIGHT PARKING PLACE helps your toddler recognize what two different objects have in common.

# FUNNY FACES

**Y**OUR TODDLER is just beginning to understand the concept of emotions—that he feels happy sometimes and perhaps angry or sad at other times. Wooden spoon puppets can help him identify and express his feelings in appropriate ways. Draw a happy face, a sad face, and a mad face on three wooden spoons. You can also dress them up with construction paper: add "hair," a "mustache," or a bow tie. Have the spoons express their "feelings" to your child or to each other. For example, the happy-face spoon can say, "Oh boy! I'm going to the zoo today!" And the mad face can say, "No! I don't want to wear my coat!" Encourage your child to express his emotions, too.

IT'S OFTEN EASIER FOR CHILDREN to express themselves through play—so let your toddler practice talking about feelings with spoon puppets.

## SKILL SPOTLIGHT

**Up until a few months ago,** your child probably had only one way of expressing "difficult" feelings: crying. Now he's getting old enough to say when he's happy, sad, or mad. Spoon puppets can model such conversations for him. Notice how he's getting rather demanding these days? Let the happy-face spoon show him how to politely ask for a glass of water instead of insisting on one.

| ✔ | Concept Development |
| ✔ | Creative Expression |
| ✔ | Language Development |
| ✔ | Social Skills |

235

# MIGHTY MEGAPHONES

## FUN WITH BOOMING VOICES

### SKILL SPOTLIGHT

**Children naturally explore** their senses during play, but this activity encourages a focused exploration of listening and making sounds. Toddlers are natural performers (hence the physical frenzy that often greets guests). Improvising with this megaphone helps turn up the volume on their creativity.

| | |
|---|---|
| **Cause and Effect** | ✔ |
| **Creative Expression** | ✔ |
| **Listening Skills** | ✔ |
| **Sensory Exploration** | ✔ |

 **HE'S SPEAKING QUITE WELL NOW,** and her vocalizations frequently range from a murmur (when she's "reading" to her teddy bear) to a shriek (when it's time to leave the playground). You can expand her verbal and auditory skills even further with a paper megaphone. Just roll up a big sheet of thick paper and show her how talking into the small end of the cone can change the tone, direction, and volume of her voice. Take turns talking loudly and softly with the megaphone, or use it for amplifying songs and silly sounds.

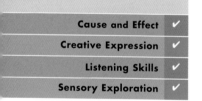

If your child enjoys this activity, also try **Animal Actors,** page 252.

NOW HEAR THIS: She'll love expanding her vocal range with this improvised amplifier.

# RIBBON RINGS

## SKILLSPOTLIGHT

**When you add ribbon rings** to a toddler's dance session, she'll become more aware of how she's moving her arms and body to make the ribbons float in different ways. This helps her develop gross motor skills and coordination. The rings also encourage rhythm exploration as well as creativity.

| | |
|---|---|
| **Body Awareness** | ✔ |
| **Coordination** | ✔ |
| **Creative Movement** | ✔ |
| **Gross Motor Skills** | ✔ |
| **Rhythm Exploration** | ✔ |

 **HE ALREADY LIKES TO DANCE,** but adding rings of colorful, floating ribbon will make her spinning and twirling all the more magical.

• Purchase a pair of ribbon rings (sold at specialty toy stores) or make your own with fabric ribbons, or strips of fabric or old sheets, that are between 12 and 25 inches (30 to 64 cm) in length. Securely tie one end of each of the ribbons or strips around small embroidery rings or canning rims.

• Talk to your child about the different colors of the ribbons and ask her to show you which one is her favorite.

• Show her how to incorporate the rings into her dance routine: wave them up and down and swing them from side to side.

• Play dancing music you both enjoy and join your toddler as she swings to the beat and makes the ribbons float and twirl.

• Put the rings on the floor and dance around them, or pass the rings back and forth as you sashay past each other. Encourage her to improvise with her pretty new props.

If your child enjoys this activity, also try **Scarf Tricks,** page 162.

A TODDLER LOVES THE COLOR, motion, and drama of rippling ribbons as they easily flutter and twirl in her hands.

# MAGNIFY MATTERS

## GETTING A BUG'S-EYE VIEW OF THE WORLD

USE A MAGNIFYING GLASS to enhance your child's curiosity about her world—and her understanding of it. She will marvel at how grains of sand look like multicolored boulders and how flat green leaves are actually etched with tiny lines.

• Take your child on a walk outdoors. Show her how to hold the magnifying glass up to different objects—such as leaves, rocks, grass, flowers, sand, even bugs—and look through it. Encourage her to touch the objects under scrutiny and help her find the appropriate words to describe what she sees.

• Talk about concepts of size ("That pebble was little until we looked at it with the magnifying glass. Now it looks really big!"). Be sure to exercise extreme caution on sunny days; when the sun's rays are shining through the magnifying glass they can burn skin or even start a fire.

• Take her for a walk indoors, too. Tell her to get an up-close view of a blanket, her toast, a houseplant, her stuffed animals, or the hair on your pet. Ask her to describe what she sees, suggesting words if she doesn't have the vocabulary.

• Use the magnifying glass to build body awareness. Let her explore her toes, fingerprints, and even your eyes and tongue.

AN ORDINARY ROCK and pinecone become intriguing landscapes of texture when your child has the chance to examine them up close and personal.

# RAIN-STICK MUSIC

## EXPLORING NATURAL SOUNDS

### SKILL SPOTLIGHT

**Back when your toddler** was a baby, a rattle was a curious toy he loved to grasp with his little fingers. Now he can experience a large "rain" rattle, which will enhance his auditory perception as he learns to listen to it and compare the sound it makes with the sound of real rain.

| Creative Movement | ✔ |
| Listening Skills | ✔ |
| Sensory Exploration | ✔ |

**T**HE LOOK AND SOUND OF RAIN fascinate most toddlers—it's water that mysteriously pours down from the sky, after all. You can re-create the sound of rain anytime with a "rain stick." Buy wooden ones at nature-oriented gift stores, or colorful plastic rain sticks at toy stores. You can also make your own rain stick by filling a poster tube with a cup of rice and securely capping both ends. Encourage your child to slowly turn his rain stick upside down while you're reading stories or singing about the rain. On stormy days, ask your toddler to listen to the real rain and then encourage him to listen to the similar sounds he can make with his special stick.

◀ If your child enjoys this activity, also try **Mystery Sounds,** page 194.

BY CREATING A SHOWER OF SOUND as he upturns his stick, he opens his senses to the world of rain and rhythm.

243

# SHAPE SORTER

## SKILL SPOTLIGHT

**This classifying game** strengthens the fundamental skills of identifying and organizing objects by a distinguishing characteristic—in this case, shape. Your toddler will also begin to understand that shapes come in many different sizes (that is, the balls are round and the bowl is round, but the bowl is the larger round object).

| | |
|---|---|
| **Classifying Skills** | ✔ |
| **Concept Development** | ✔ |
| **Size and Shape Discrimination** | ✔ |

**T**HIS QUICK AND EASY ACTIVITY helps children learn to organize different shapes. Simply collect an assortment of small balls and square-shaped blocks and mix them up in a pile. Put out a large bowl and a big box. Ask your child to place all of the round balls in the round bowl and the blocks in the box. It may take a few tries, but with your help he'll soon be sorting the shapes into the correct containers with ease.

If your child enjoys this activity, also try **Leaf Lineup,** page 248.

PUTTING ROUND OBJECTS and square-shaped blocks into larger, similarly shaped containers helps your child sort out the differences among shapes and sizes.

30 MONTHS
2½
AND UP

LOOKING FOR "ONE MORE" introduces the concept of numbers into the treasure hunt.

# COUNT AND SEEK

**Y**OUNG CHILDREN OF ALL AGES love finding a hidden object—whether it's a baby's rattle, Mommy's face, or a cookie hidden in Daddy's pocket. Asking a child to find more than one object adds counting practice to the fun. Simply collect three or more similar items such as cups, shoes, wooden spoons, or colored balls. Show the items to your toddler, hide them around the house (be sure you leave a part of the "hidden" objects exposed so your child can find them more readily), and then ask him to search for them. Count out loud to tally the objects he finds and applaud every time he finds one. To make the game harder, hide more matching objects.

If your child enjoys this activity, also try **Flashlight Fun,** page 206.

### SKILL SPOTLIGHT

**Finding the objects** will boost your child's self-esteem (so don't hide the objects too well). Counting aloud as he finds them will help him learn both the sequence of numbers and an elementary concept of addition. The challenge of finding an object that he saw just a few moments ago also helps build his visual memory.

✔ **Counting Concepts**

✔ **Visual Discrimination**

✔ **Visual Memory**

# LEAF LINEUP

## SKILL SPOTLIGHT

**Categorizing things** is immensely interesting for toddlers because it's a way of organizing and even controlling the world around them. This activity lets them learn the concepts of big and small and practice identifying which objects are which size. Talking about leaves also teaches children the words for colors and sizes and gives them a brief nature lesson.

| | |
|---|---|
| **Classifying Skills** | ✔ |
| **Concept Development** | ✔ |
| **Language Development** | ✔ |
| **Size and Shape Discrimination** | ✔ |

**Y**OUR CHILD IS QUITE INTENT on identifying his possessions ("That's my spoon!") and sorting them into various categories ("These are my hats. These are my shoes."). Take advantage of his dual love of possessions and sorting by creating a leaf collection. Gather small, medium, and large leaves. Tape one example of each size onto the sides of paper bags or small boxes. Place the rest of the leaves in a pile. Ask your child to sort the leaves into the correct bag or box according to size. While he sorts, talk to him about the leaves—where they came from, for instance, and their colors. Having a hard time finding leaves? Cut out some leaf shapes from colored construction paper.

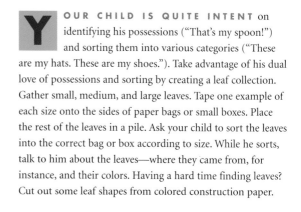

WHAT GOES WHERE? Sorting a leaf collection is a great way to expand his understanding of big, medium, and small.

# COPYCAT

## SKILLSPOTLIGHT

**Children learn** by observing others—especially their parents. This wonderfully interactive activity is a good way to show your child day-to-day chores (although she's not ready to be assigned large tasks yet). It also boosts her confidence as she pretends to accomplish what Mommy and Daddy do. Imitating your voice and gestures builds auditory and visual skills; doing it to the beat of music also helps her explore rhythm.

| | |
|---|---|
| **Coordination** | ✔ |
| **Gross Motor Skills** | ✔ |
| **Listening Skills** | ✔ |
| **Role-Playing** | ✔ |
| **Social Skills** | ✔ |

**S**HE'S CARRYING YOUR HANDBAG and talking to the pets the same way you do. Sometimes it's delightful and sometimes it's embarrassing: do you really say, "Get down!" in that tone of voice? Now make imitation a joint activity— and try to get some chores done in the process.

• Encourage your child to "help" you rake leaves, dust, sweep, or build a birdhouse. You can give her tot-size tools or safe adult ones, or just let her perform her tasks with make-believe supplies. She'll love giving you a helping hand.

• If you have a family pet, ask your child to help feed, exercise, groom, or play with it. She'll learn new skills, including how to nurture the animal just as you nurture her.

• A garden is an ideal place for a child to help. Demonstrate how to plant seeds, then let her try. When the planting is long forgotten and the first shoots come up, you can surprise your young gardener by showing her the fruits of her labor.

• Adding music to your projects is a great way to enhance any task—especially if you whistle (or sing) while you work.

DUST BUSTING is a chore toddlers adore, so let your little helper make this task more fun for you—and let her know that her work is appreciated.

## RESEARCH REPORT

**Many parents are surprised** at the gusto a young child will bring to everyday activities such as sweeping the floor or sponging off a counter. Yet almost a century ago, an Italian physician and educator named Maria Montessori trumpeted the value of meaningful chores—among many other revolutionary notions about early childhood. She said such chores help promote a child's sense of responsibility and self-esteem, and allow her to feel like she's contributing to the family or classroom. Today at the thousands of schools worldwide where teaching is based on Montessori's theories, classrooms are stocked with low-standing sinks, pint-size brooms and mops, and other cleaning supplies, and even the youngest preschoolers are expected to help.

251

# ANIMAL ACTORS

## IMITATING THE ANIMAL WORLD

## SKILL SPOTLIGHT

**It takes balance,** strength, and even coordination to stalk like a lion, to sweep a "trunk" along the ground, or to mimic a bird flying above the treetops. Pretending to be an animal also gives wings to your child's imagination and helps her develop empathy for other creatures in the world.

| | |
|---|---|
| **Concept Development** | ✔ |
| **Creative Movement** | ✔ |
| **Gross Motor Skills** | ✔ |
| **Imagination** | ✔ |

**S**HE BARKS AT THE DOG and crawls alongside the cat. Going to the zoo makes her zany with excitement. Toddlers adore animals and the funny ways they move and "speak." Help your child explore the beauty of beasts by teaching her how to mimic them.

• Begin by looking at animal pictures in books and magazines with your toddler and talking about their behavior—how they walk, what they eat, where they live, and the ways they communicate. Also assemble her stuffed animals and explain what life would be like for them if they were real creatures.

• Demonstrate the sounds each animal makes: the bear growls, the cat meows, the rooster crows, and the frog croaks. Then ask your child to roar, purr, or "ribbit" like the animals she sees at the park or in cartoons, in videos, or at the zoo.

• Show her the actions of various animals: a duck waddles, a horse trots, a frog hops from lily pad to lily pad, a monkey swings from branch to branch, and an elephant uses its trunk to pull leaves from the trees. Ask her to waddle, trot, jump, swing her arms, and stretch the same way the animals do.

YOUR LITTLE MONKEY enhances her imagination and physical agility as she apes the animals she sees.

# GLOSSARY

## A

### ABSTRACT THOUGHT
The ability to imagine and discuss people, ideas, and objects when they are not physically present. Pretending, notions of time, finding a lost object, and making plans to visit a friend all require some degree of abstract thought.

### AUDITORY DEVELOPMENT
The auditory system's maturation, which is necessary for spoken language development.

## B

### BALANCE
The ability to assume and maintain body positions against the force of gravity. A sense of balance is crucial for learning how to sit, stand, walk, run, jump, skate, and ride a bike.

### BILATERAL COORDINATION
The ability to use both sides of the body simultaneously, whether or not the movements are symmetrical. A child needs bilateral coordination to crawl, walk, swim, climb, catch, and jump.

### BODY AWARENESS
A person's understanding of what limbs, joints, and muscles feel like as well as his ability to locate his own body parts.

## C

### CAUSE AND EFFECT
How one action affects another. Experience with cause and effect helps a child learn how her actions create a result.

### CLASSIFYING SKILLS
The ability to group objects according to a common characteristic, such as size, shape, or color.

### COGNITION
Mental or intellectual abilities, including recognizing, classifying, and comparing objects; remembering routines, people, and object placement; making judgments; and solving problems.

### CONCEPT AWARENESS
An understanding of specific concepts, such as open/closed and big/little.

### COORDINATION

The ability to integrate all of the senses to produce a movement response that is smooth, efficient, and skillful, such as kicking a ball.

### COUNTING CONCEPTS

The ability to recite numbers in the correct order and to recognize one-to-one correspondence.

### CREATIVE EXPRESSION

Using voice, movement, or art (such as painting or drawing) to communicate feelings and ideas.

### CREATIVE MOVEMENT

Using bodily motion (such as imitating animals or dancing) to communicate feelings and ideas.

# D

### DENDRITES

Branching nerve cells that carry nerve impulses within the brain. Researchers believe that mental stimulation increases the size and complexity of dendrite networks, which consequently improves a child's cognition.

# GLOSSARY

## E

### EYE-FOOT COORDINATION

Gauging distance and depth with the eyes and processing that information to coordinate when and where to place the feet. Eye-foot coordination is required, for example, when kicking a ball or walking on an uneven path.

### EYE-HAND COORDINATION

Directing the position and motion of the hands (when tossing or catching a ball, for instance) in response to visual information.

## F

### FINE MOTOR SKILLS

Control of the small muscles, especially those in the hands, to execute small movements, such as picking up a raisin, cutting with scissors, writing, and using buttons, snaps, and shoelaces.

## G

### GROSS MOTOR SKILLS

Control of the large muscles, such as those in the arms and legs. Gross motor activities include walking, running, and climbing.

## I

### IMAGINATION

The ability to form mental images of what is not present. Imagination involves the act of creating new ideas by combining past experiences. It also involves abstract thought. Imagination enables a child to practice roles and create new scenarios.

## L

### LANGUAGE DEVELOPMENT
The complex process of acquiring language skills, including understanding human speech, producing sounds and spoken language, and learning how to read and write.

### LISTENING SKILLS
The ability to discern various sounds, including music, rhythm, and pitch, as well as the intonation of spoken language.

### LOGICAL REASONING
The ability to make decisions or take actions based on an understood progression of facts or physical characteristics. Sorting, nesting, and stacking objects depend on logical reasoning. A toddler's understanding that she needs to drag a chair over to her father's desk in order to reach his computer also shows logical reasoning.

## N

### NEURONS
Long nerve cells that carry electrical impulses throughout the body. Different kinds of nerve cells enable us to move our bodies, think, use our senses, and experience emotions.

## P

### PROBLEM SOLVING
The ability to work out a solution to a mental or physical puzzle. A toddler solves a problem when he figures out how to screw a lid on a jar or pick up his cup without letting go of his stuffed animal.

## R

### REFLEXES
Automatic responses to stimuli and events (for example, putting your hand up to stop a ball from hitting you).

### RHYTHM EXPLORATION
The act of exploring the rhythms and underlying beat of music through movement.

### ROLE-PLAYING
Using the imagination to pretend that you are someone or something else. Role-playing can help a child explore her feelings.

## S

**SELF-CONCEPT**
A child's understanding that he is an individual person. A child who has a good self-concept feels good about himself.

**SENSORY EXPLORATION**
Using the senses of touch, hearing, sight, smell, and taste to learn about the world.

**SHAPE RECOGNITION**
The ability to identify specific forms, such as circles and triangles. Shape recognition eventually helps a child learn to read and write.

**SIZE AND SHAPE DISCRIMINATION**
The ability to identify objects of different dimensions and their relationship to each other, such as "the big dog" or "the square box."

**SOCIAL SKILLS**
Interacting and relating appropriately to other people, including sharing, taking turns, and recognizing other people's emotions.

**SPATIAL AWARENESS**
Knowing where one's own body is in relation to other people and objects. A child uses spatial awareness to crawl under a bed, walk through doorways, and generally move through space.

**SYNAPSES**
The tiny gaps between neurons through which electrical impulses jump, thus allowing nerve cells to communicate with one another.

## T

**TACTILE DISCRIMINATION**
The ability to determine differences in shape or texture by touch. Being able to discern textures helps children explore and understand their environment and recognize objects.

**TACTILE STIMULATION**
Input to receptors that respond to pressure, temperature, pain, and the movement of hairs on the skin. Tactile stimulation enables a child to feel comfortable with new experiences such as first foods and unexpected touch.

# U

## UPPER-BODY STRENGTH

The development of muscles in the arms, neck, shoulders, and upper trunk. Developing upper-body strength is crucial to crawling, pulling up, and carrying heavy objects.

# V

## VISUAL DISCRIMINATION

The ability to focus on and distinguish objects within a visual field. A toddler uses visual dis-crimination to find a bird in a picture or locate a parent in a crowd of people.

## VISUAL MEMORY

The ability to recall objects, faces, and images. Visual memory allows a child to remember a sequence of objects or pictures. It also serves as a foundation for learning to read.

# SKILLS INDEX

continued ▶

# SKILLS INDEX

# SKILLS INDEX

# INDEX

# INDEX

# ACKNOWLEDGMENTS

**A VERY SPECIAL THANKS** to all the children, parents, and grandparents featured in this book:

Robin & Jessica Alvarado
Eric Anderson
José & Anna Arcellana
Lisa & Summer Atwood
Debbie & Karly Baker
Madeleine Barnum
Leticia & Mikailah Bassard
Dana & Nicholas Bisconti
Annamaria & Sean
  Mireles Boulton
Catherine & Lizzie Boyle
Jackson Breuner-Brooks
Ashley Bryant
Madison Carbone
Christian Chubbs
Jamila Coleman
Kevin & Sofia Colosimo
Kim & Katherine Daifotis
Jane & Robert Davis
Keeson Davis
Kimberly & Jacob Dreyer
Margaret & Lauren
  Dunlap
Stacy, Sydney & Sophie
  Dunne
Tiffany & Simon Eng
Edgar & Melanie Estonina
Christina Fallone

Kristen & Kaitlin Fenn &
  Susan Carlson
Terri & Jacob Giamartino
Sharon & Annabel
  Gonzalez
Carrie Green-Zinn &
  Zaria Zinn
Jade & Jordan Greene
Annette, Katie & Connor
  Hagan
Drew Harris
Arthur & Reed
  Haubenstock
Cameron & Bix Hirigoyen
Laurasia Holzman-Smith
Rochelle Jackson
Ryan Jahabli-Danekas
David Johnson
Lynne Jowett & Eloise
  Shaw
Elana Kalish
Gilda & Megan Kan
Caecilia Kim & Addison
  Brenneman
Olivier & Raphael Laude
Mark & Samantha Leeper
Mary & Simon Lindsay
Darien & Nicholas Lum

Peg Mallery & Elliot Dean
Ryan McCarty
Susan McKeever & Sophia
  Rosney
Alex Mellin
Justin Miloslavich
Lou, Terri & Lou Molinaro
Tom, Genevieve &
  Graham Morgan
Madeleine Myall
Betsy & Megumi
  Nakamura
Abby Newbold
Carly Olson
Terry, Kim & Hunter
  Patterson
Elizabeth & Hayden Payne
Henrietta & Katie Plessas
Bronwyn & Griffin Posynick
Jim & Kira Pusch
Shanti Rachlis
Wayne & Thomas Riley
Kali Roberts
Blake Rotter
Leigh & Kai Sata
Haley Shipway
Kathryn Siegler
David Sparks

Jackie & Jaylyn Stemple
Brisa & Diva Stevens
Eloisa Tejero & Isabella
  Shin
Alisa & David Tomlinson
Lila & April Torres
Mahsati & Kiana Tsao
Paula Venables
Sebastian & Julian von
  Nagel
Gabriel Wanderley
Jenifer Warren & Grace
  Bailey
Pernille & Sebastian
  Wilkenschildt
Daisy & Karinna Wong
Sara Wong & Dean &
  Jack Fukushima
Tina & Anna Wood
Amy & Marissa Wright
Jill & Nicole Zanolli
Lisa Zuniga & Maria
  Carlsen

*Mirror on page 80 from Mudpie in San Francisco. Crayola and serpentine design are registered trademarks of Binney & Smith and are used with permission.*